this buk belongs to-

age-

adres-

i lov americer

tony & me

by
georg bush

as told to dr parsons

scribner

1st publishd in grate briten by Scribner in 2002. an imprint of simon & shuster UK Ltd. a viacom cumpny.

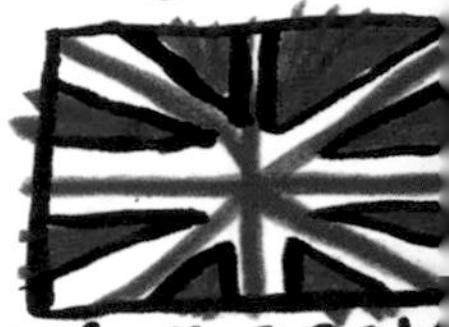

wat a grat
cuntr

3 5 7 9 10 8 6 4

Simon & shuster UK Ltd
africa hous
64-78 kingsway
Londun
WC2B 6AH

www.simonsays.co.uk

simon & shuster Australya - Sidney
a CIP catalog for this buk is avaylabl from the british libry

isbn 0-7432-3962-8

printed + bownd in grate briten by butler and tanner Lt

this buk is a wurk of ficshunl satire altho referenses to acshual persons ar included, such persons appear in ficshunlis insidents and any resemblans to acshual events or localitys is entirely coinsidental

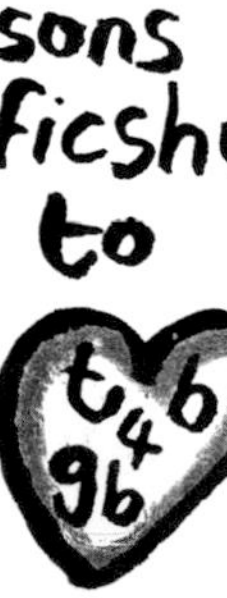

georg bush wuld like to thank enron, wurldcom, esso, monsanto, andersen, the big oyl guys, the texas ranjers, utimco, daddi, god, my bisnis pardners an corprat doners (espeshly the tobaco compnys), the 'guys' who bort my shares in Harken enerji, pepsi for throwin all those partis for me, an all the gud wite peopl of americer

Dr Parsons would like to thank all the faithful crazies: Laurence, Emma, Pussy, Gosh, Rough Trade, Page 45, skeletor, Alistram, Andrew, and all the Americans who wrote me angry emails about my website. ∇§

my name is georg bush an im presidant of americer.

this is a pitur of me

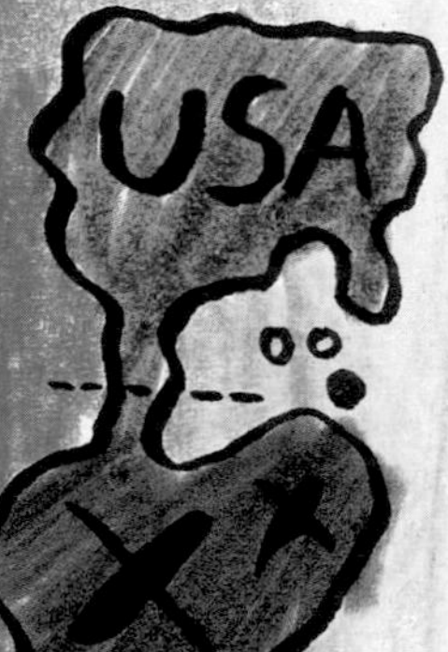
USA

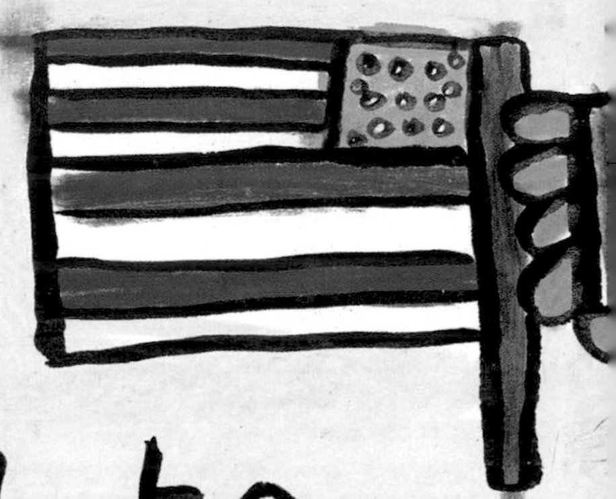

i get to wear a tie evry day

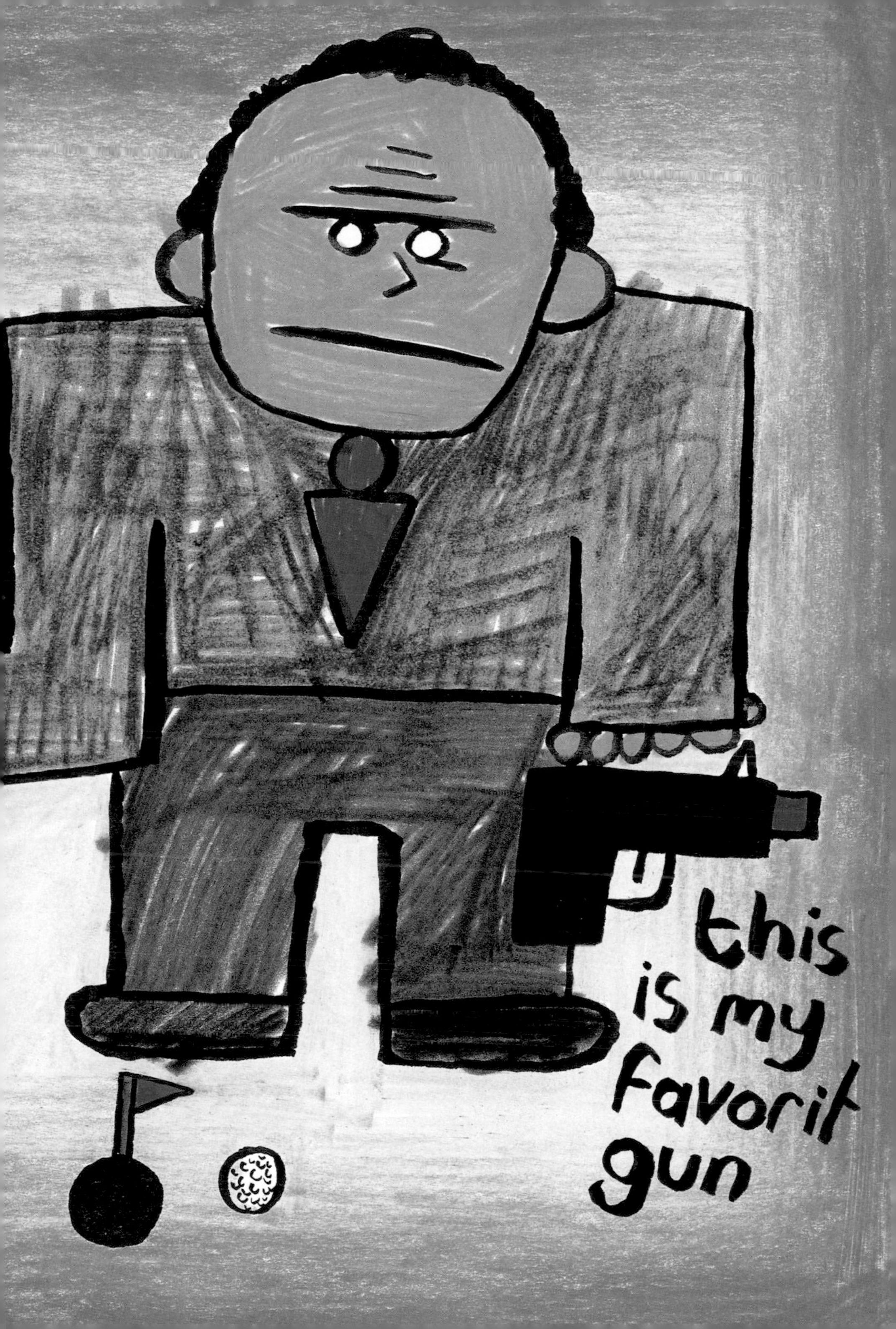
this
is my
favorit
gun

these ar my speshl

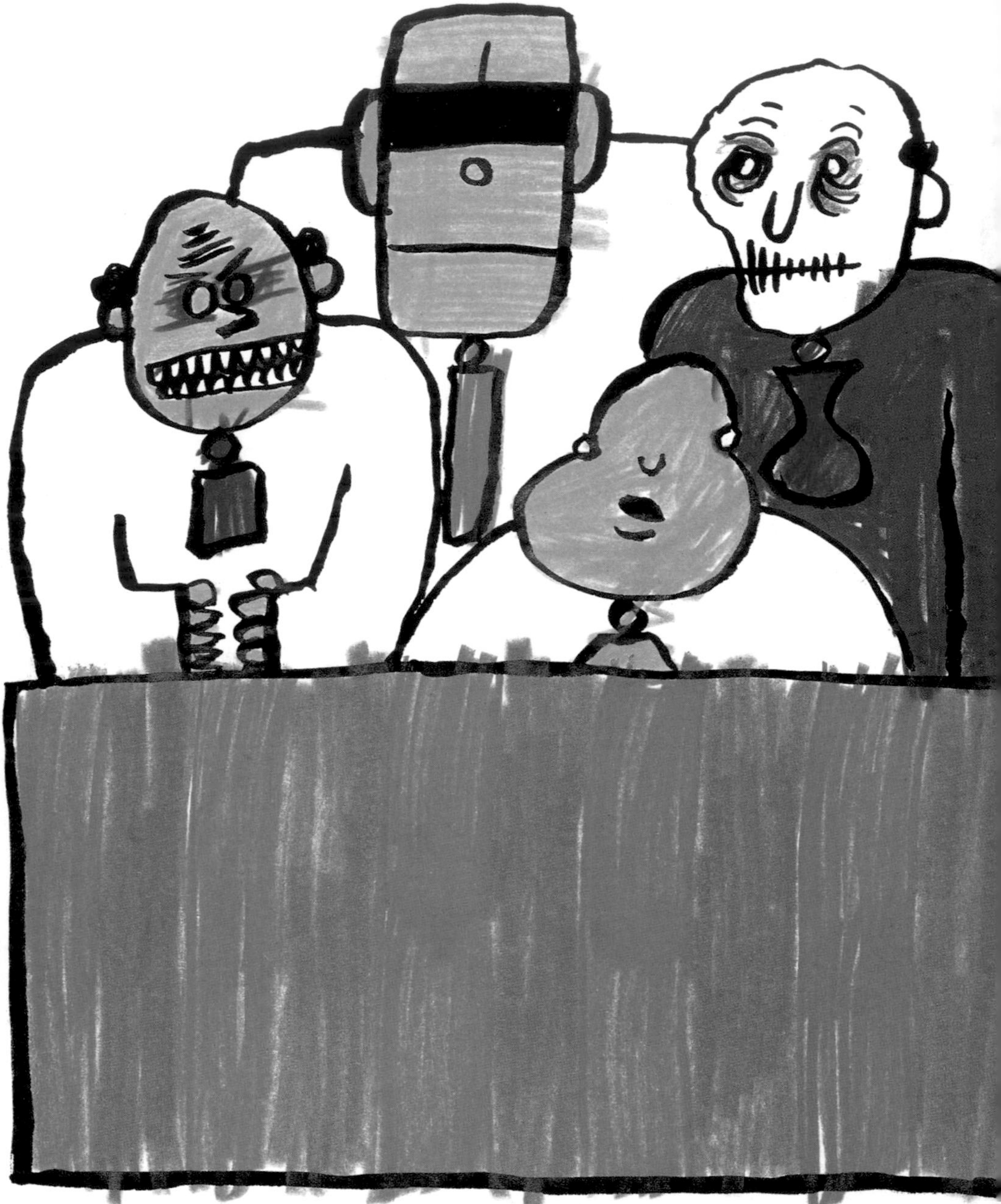

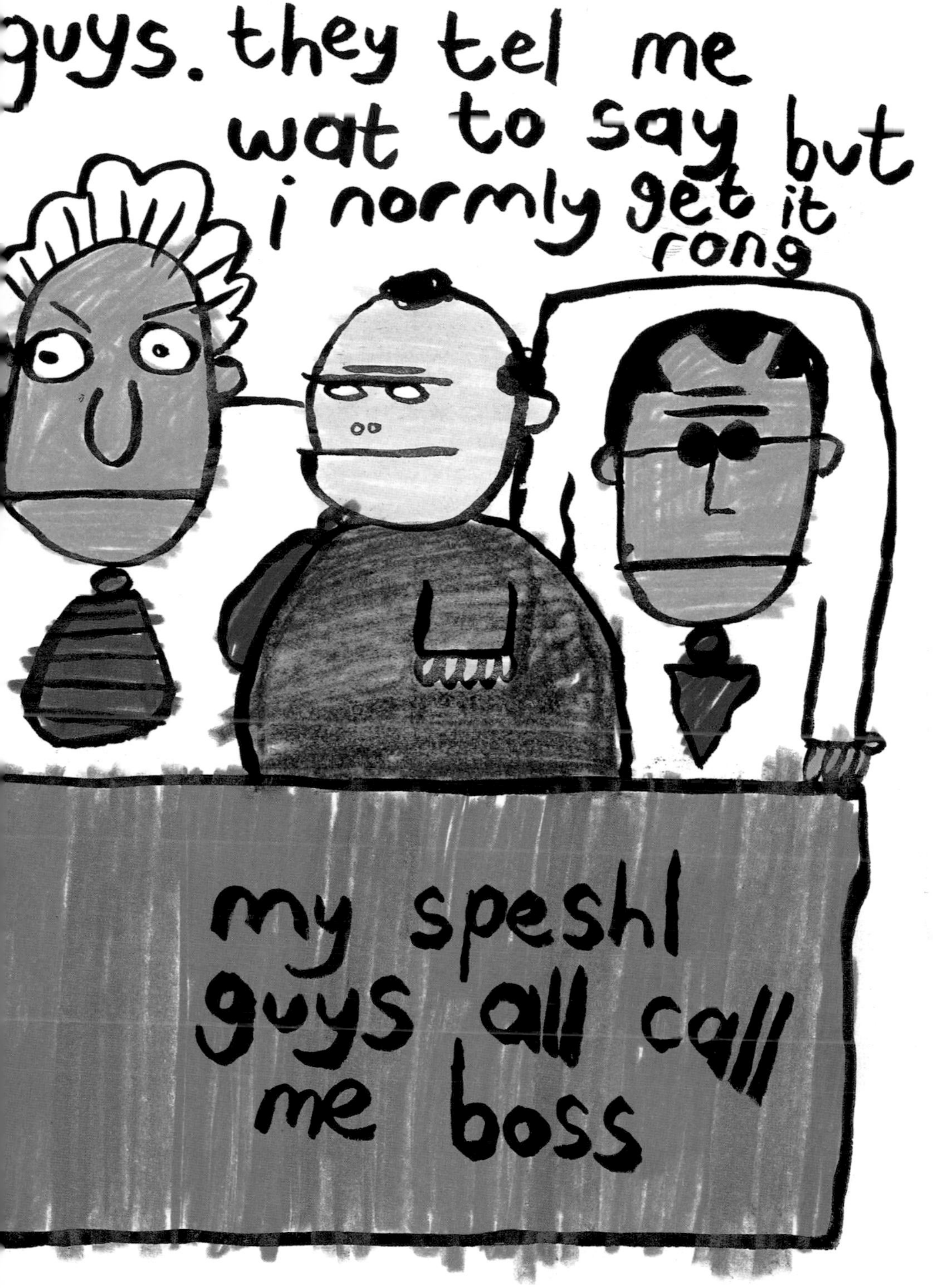
guys. they tel me wat to say but i normly get it rong
my speshl guys all call me boss

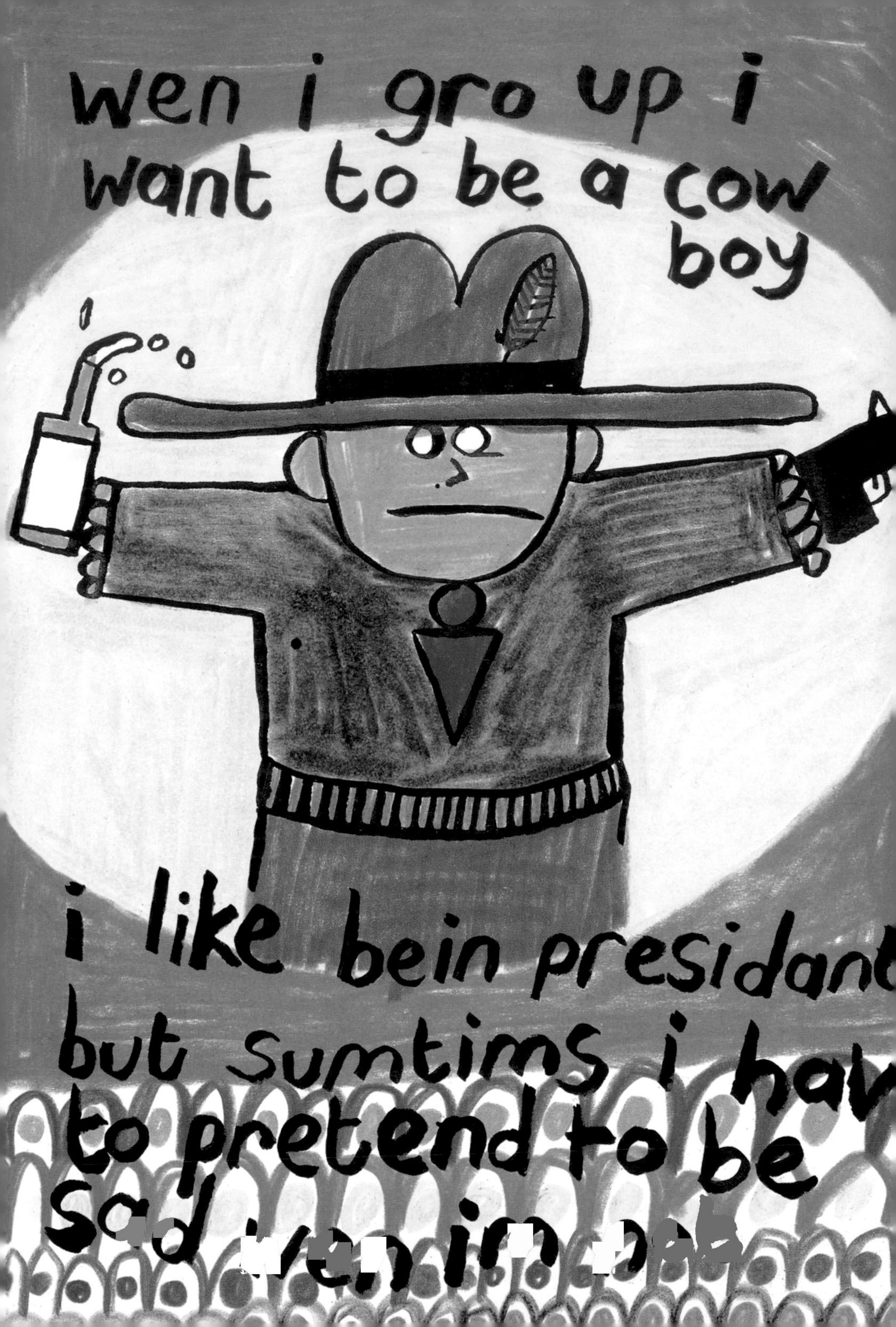
wen i gro up i
want to be a cow
boy
i like bein presidant
but sumtims i hav
to pretend to be
sad

i have the most guns
playns boms an soljers
in the wurld

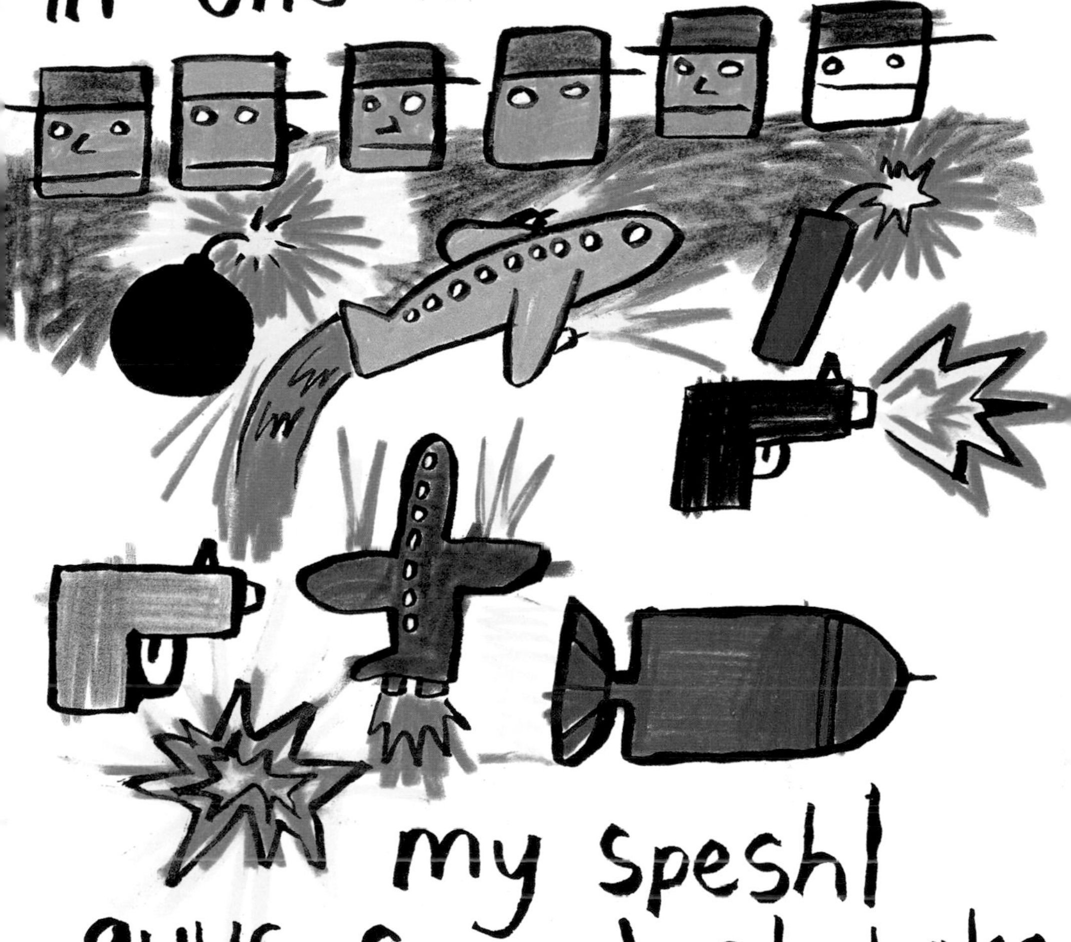

my speshl
guys say dont take
shit from noone

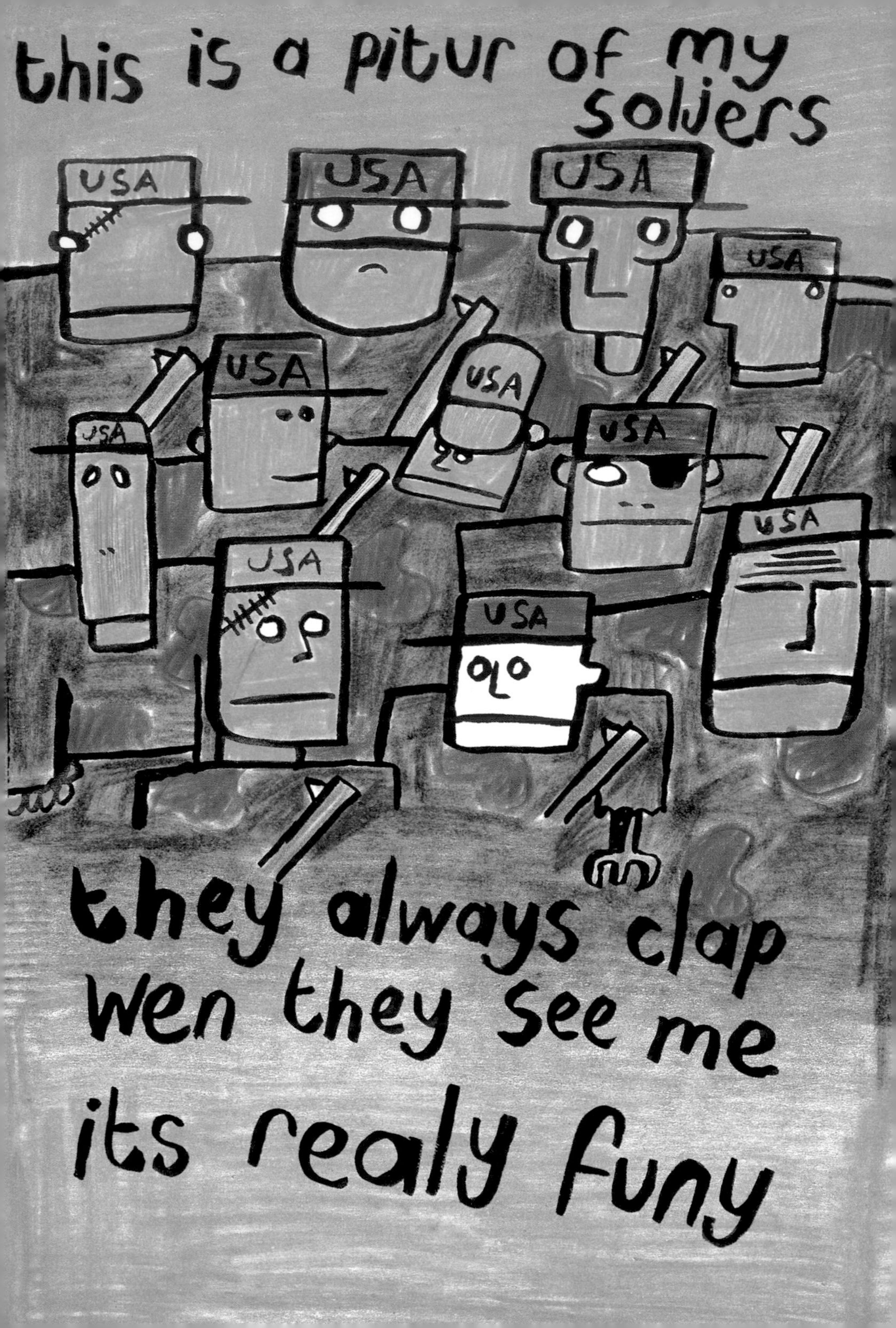
this is a pitur of my soljers
they always clap wen they see me
its realy funy

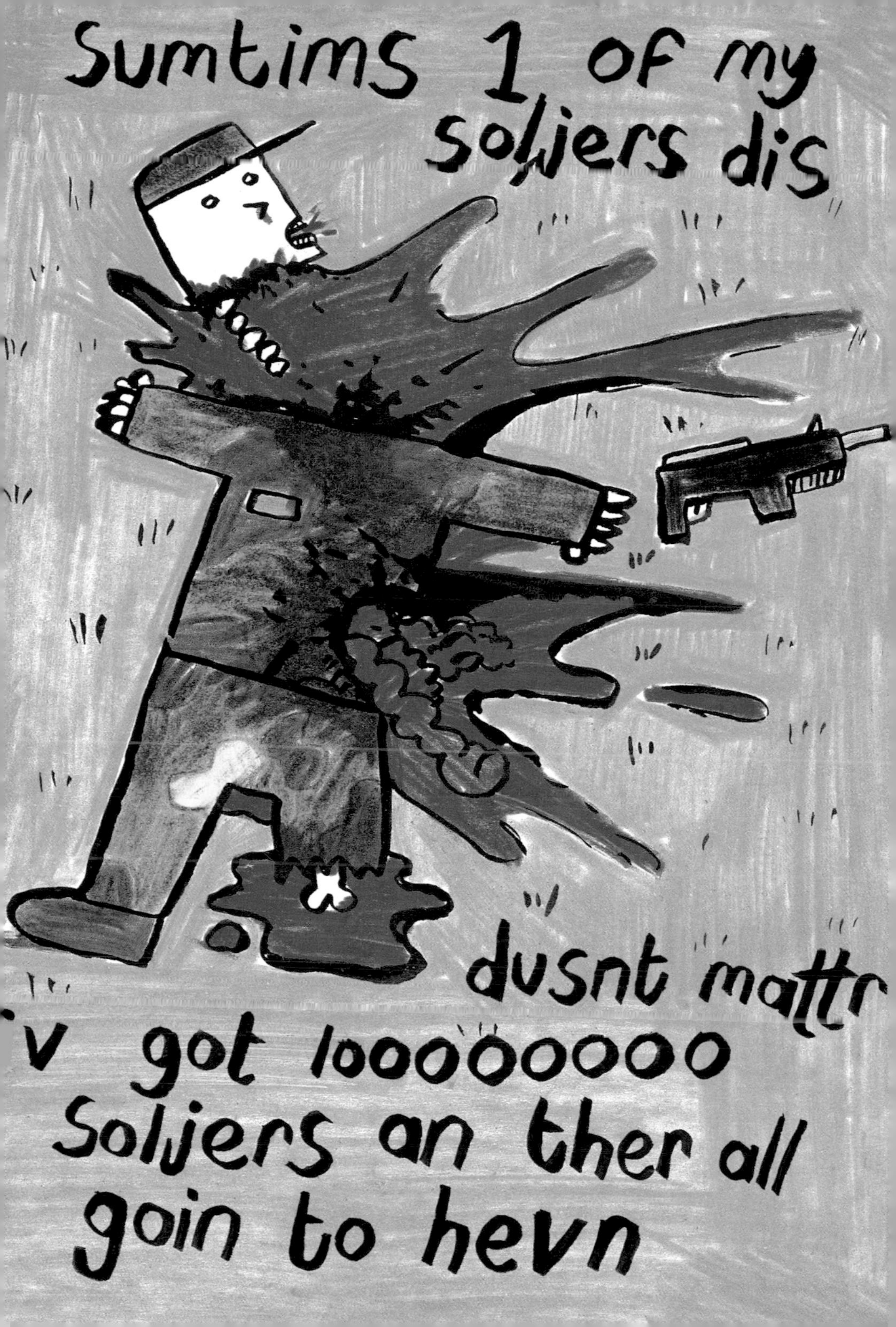

Sumtims 1 of my soljers dis
dusnt mattr
'v got 100000000 soljers an ther all goin to hevn

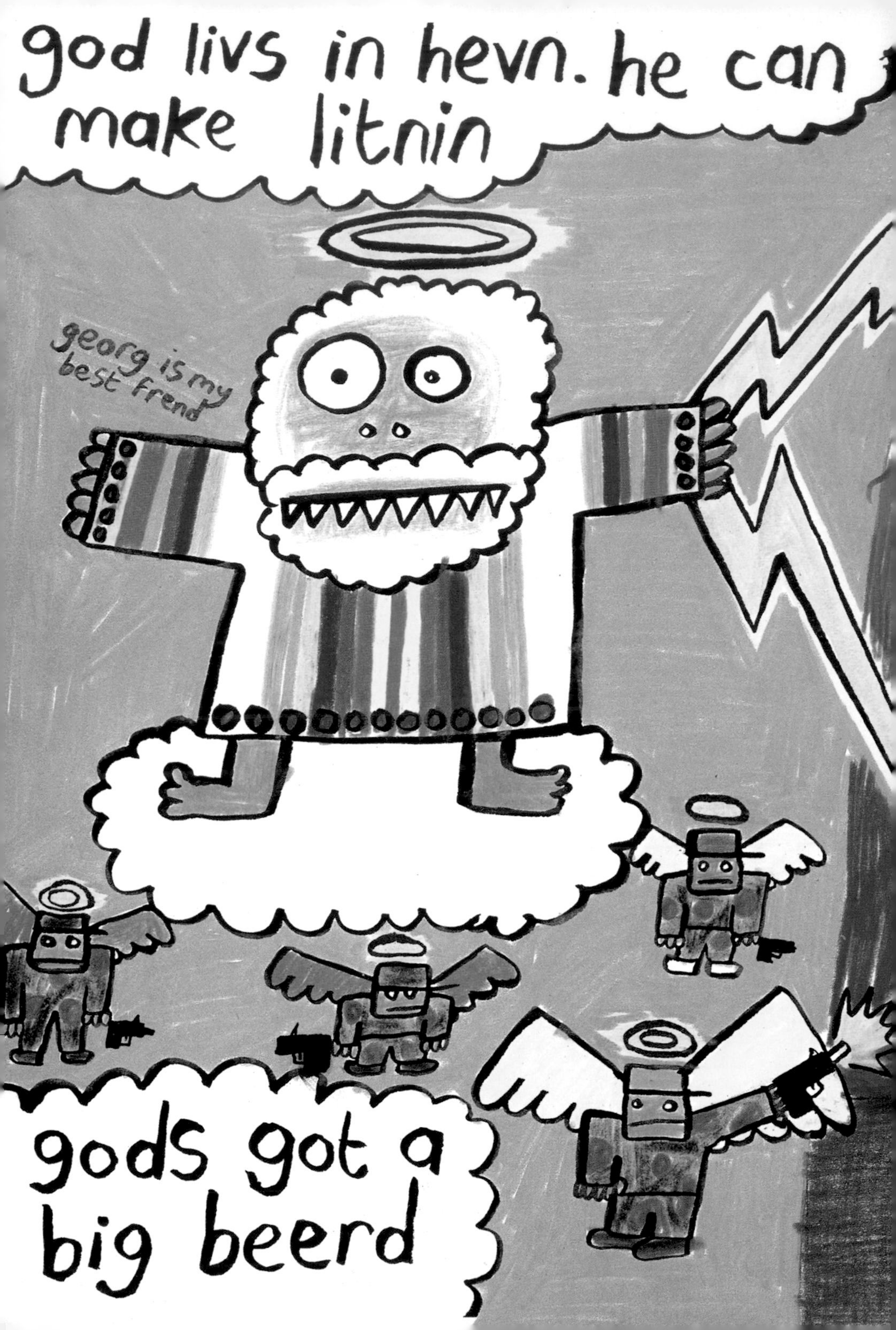
god livs in hevn. he can make litnin
georg is my best frend
gods got a big beerd

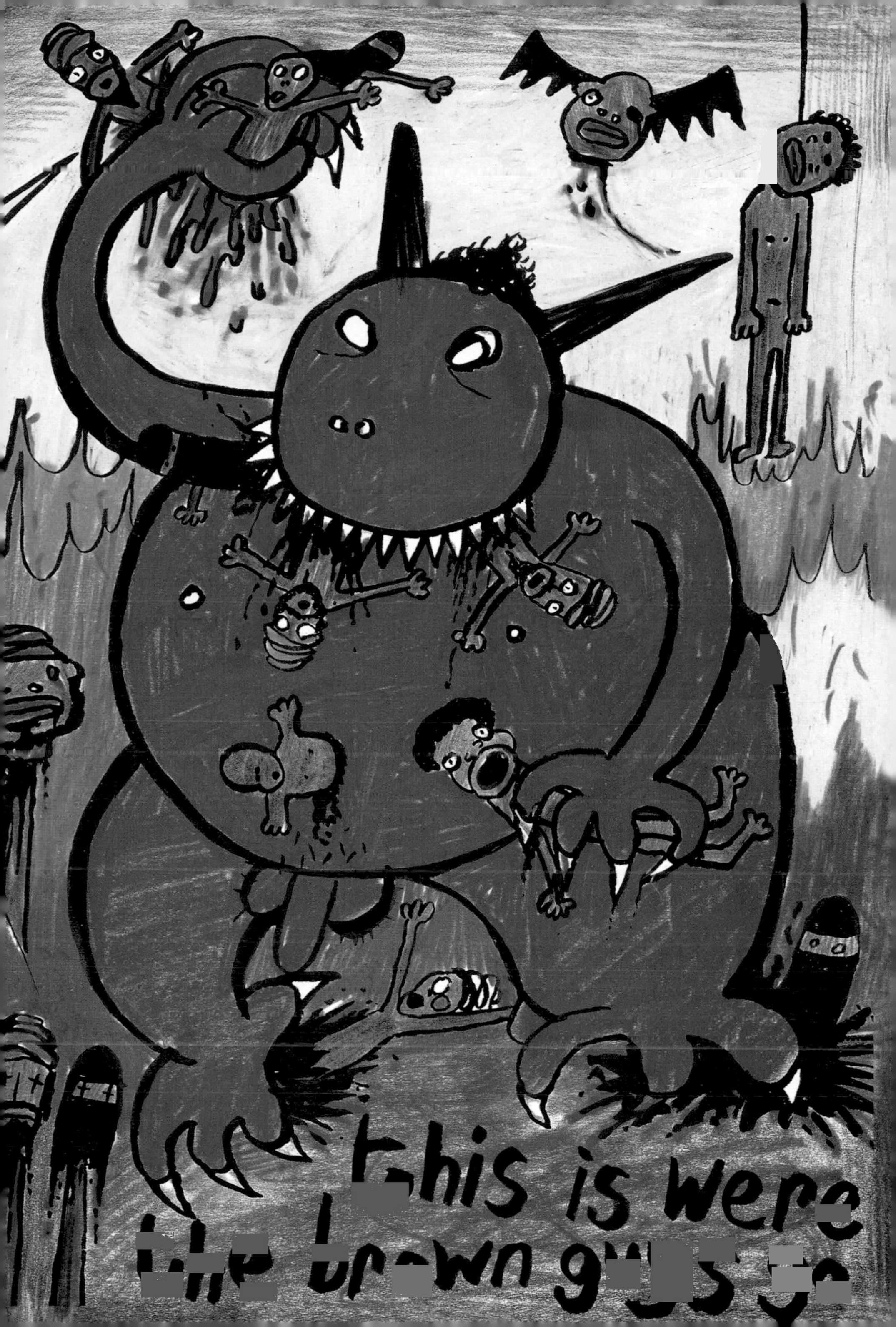
this is were

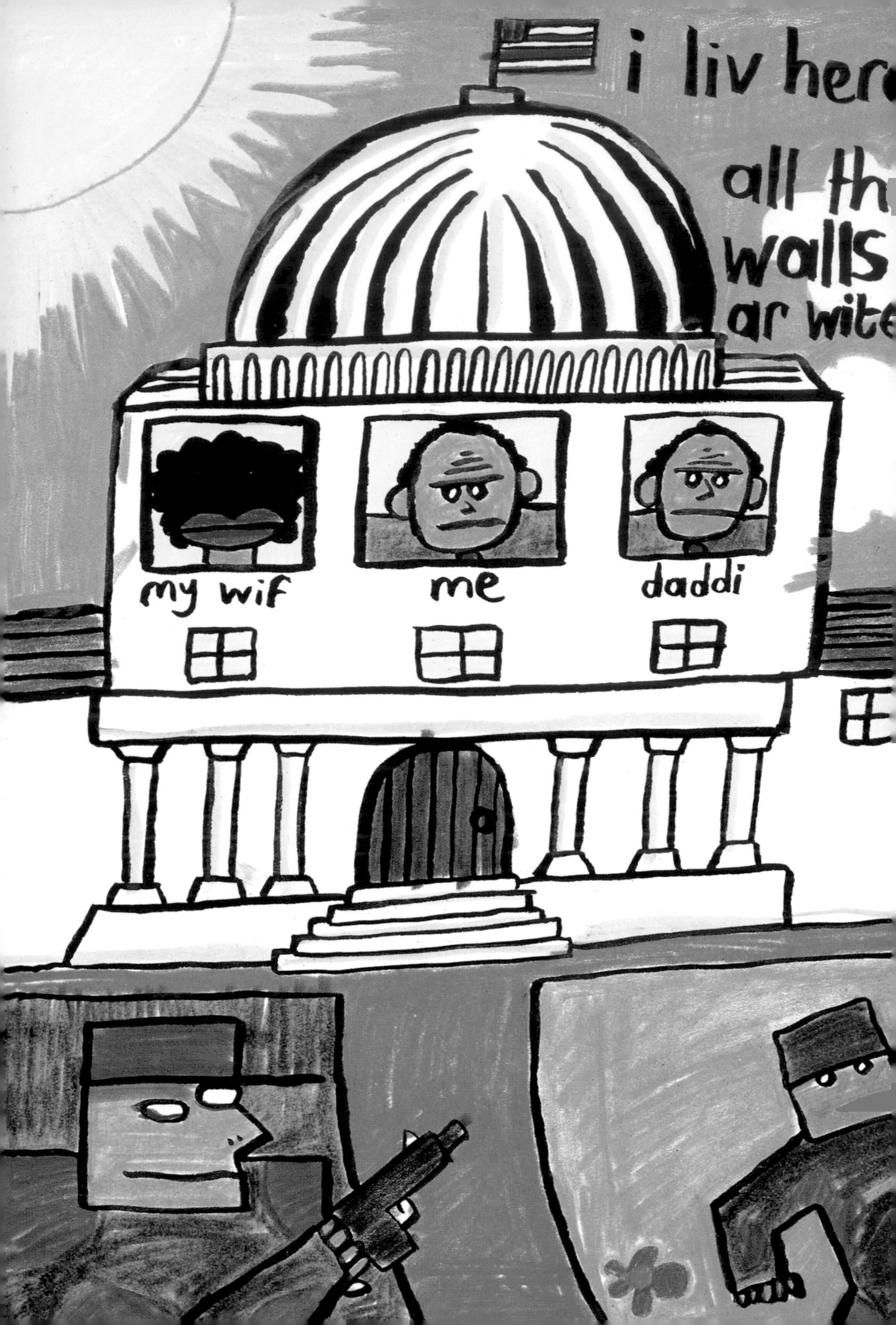

i liv her
all th
walls
ar wite
my wif
me
daddi

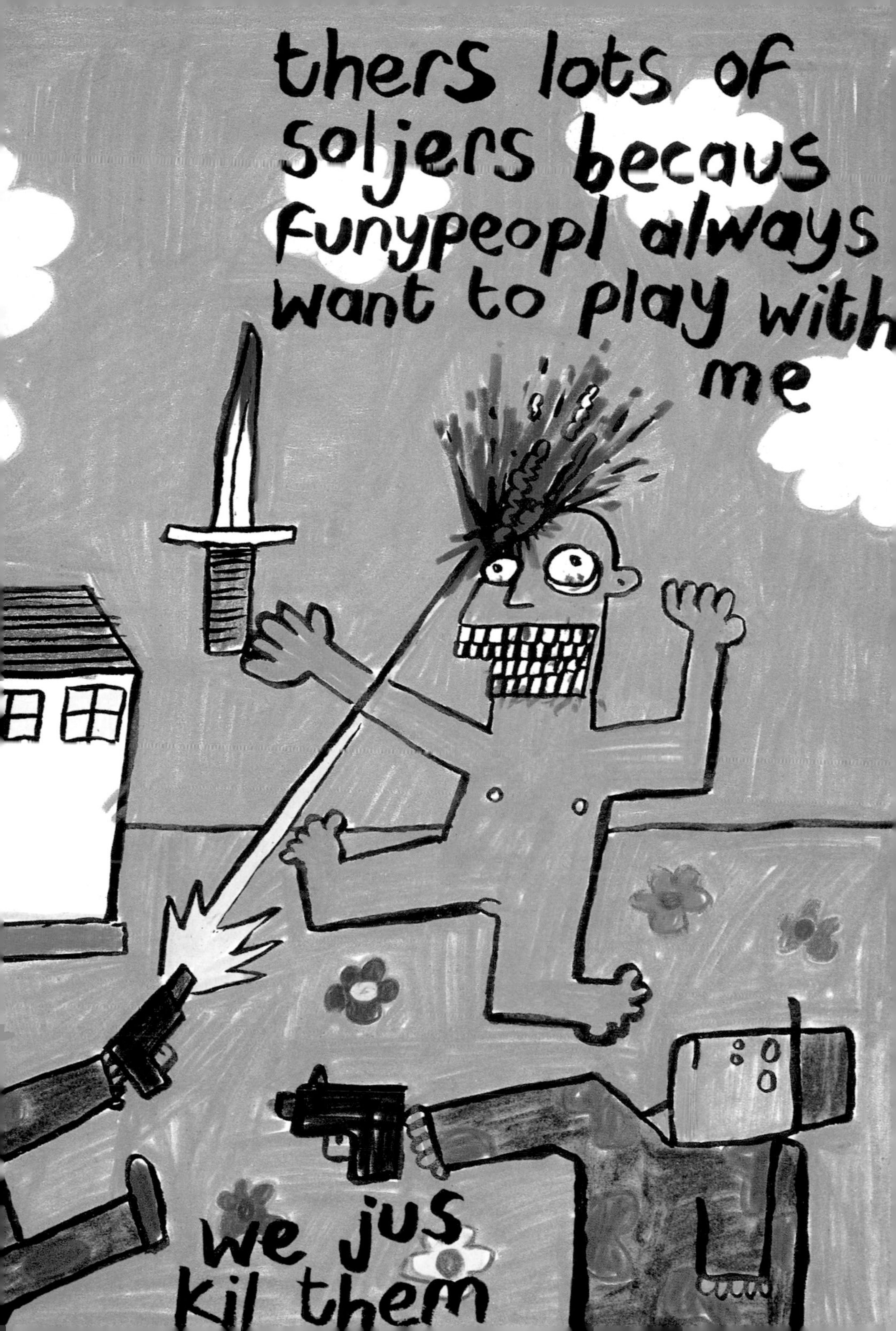
thers lots of soljers becaus funypeopl always want to play with me
we jus kil them

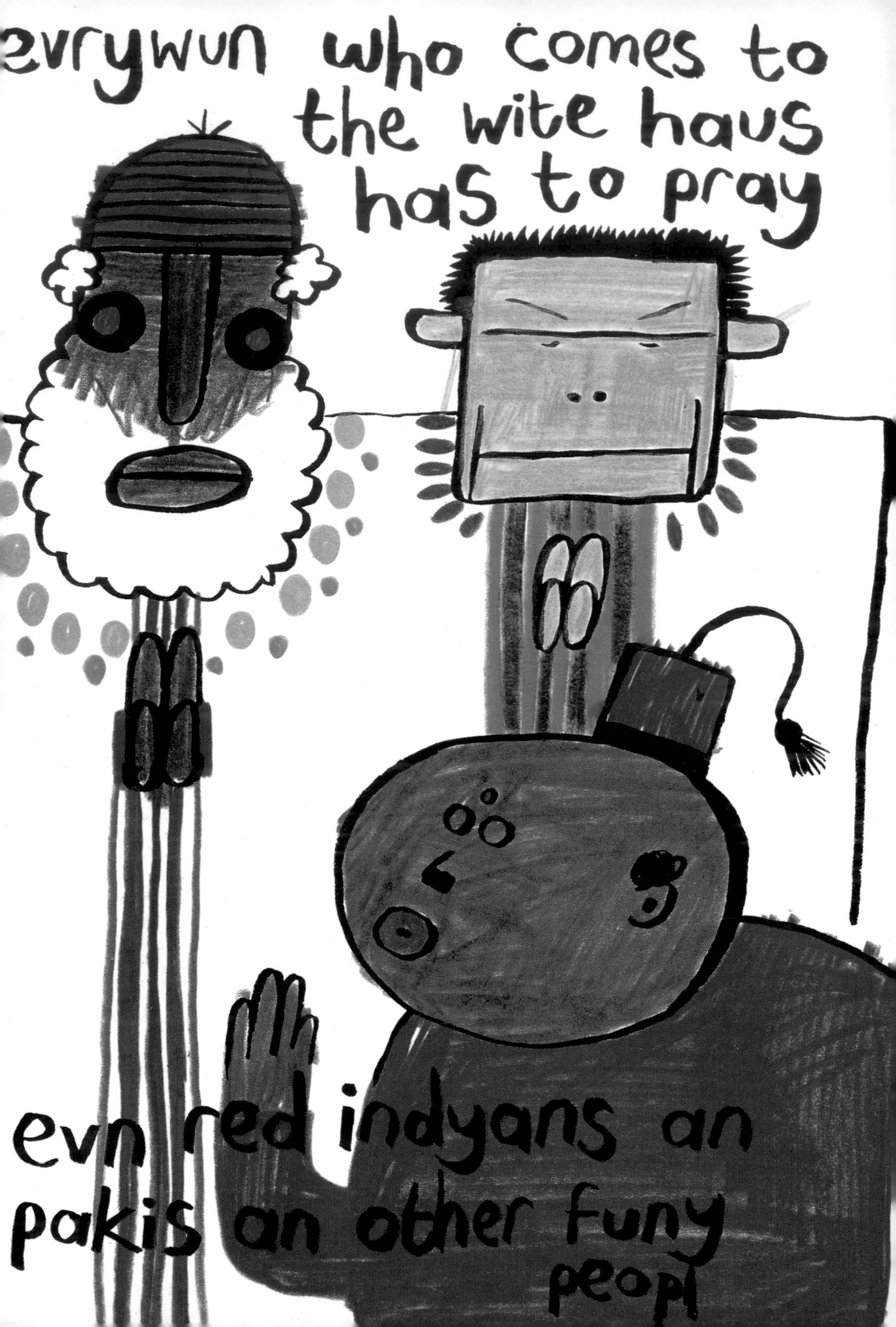
evrywun who comes to the wite haus has to pray
evn red indyans an pakis an other funy peopl

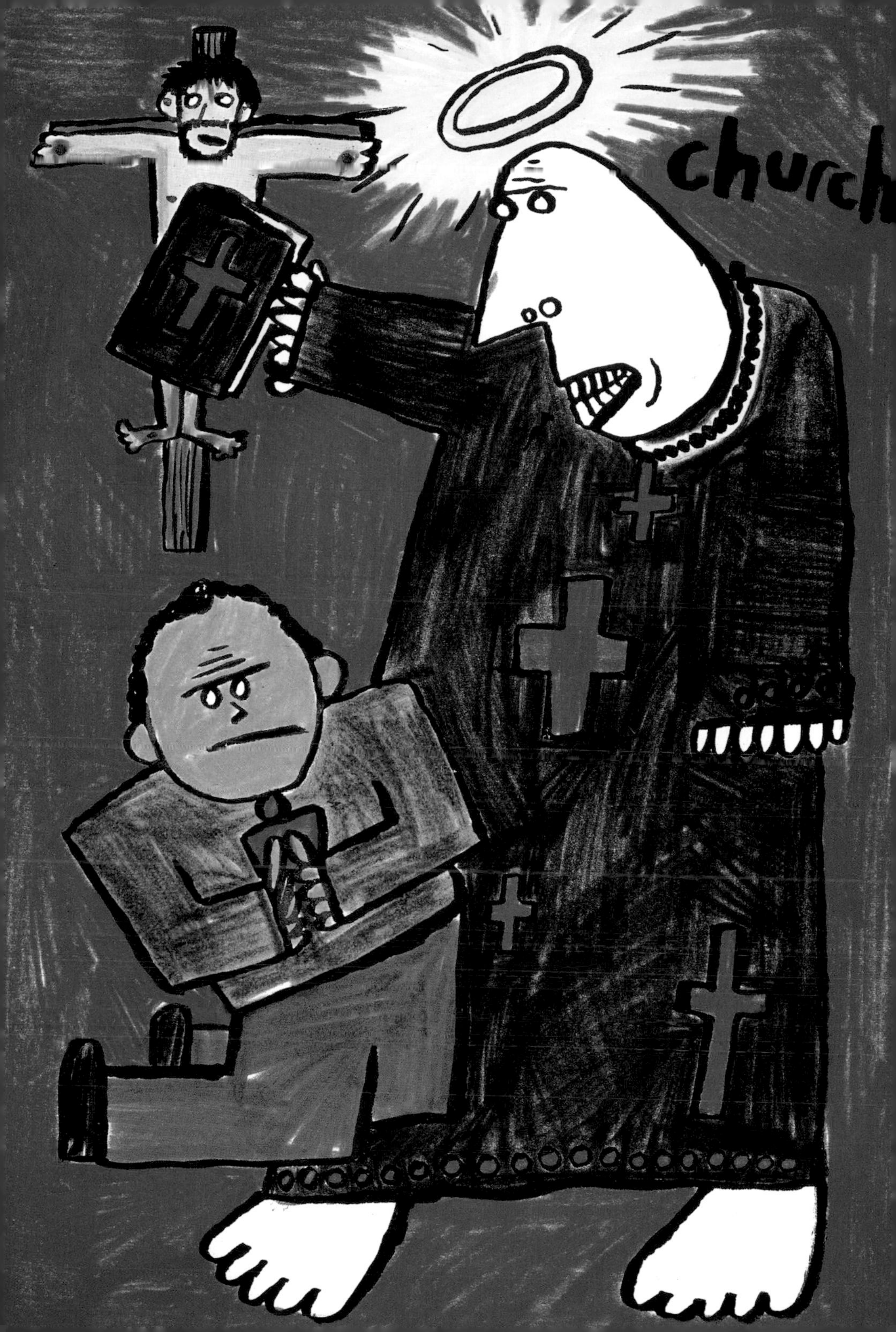
church

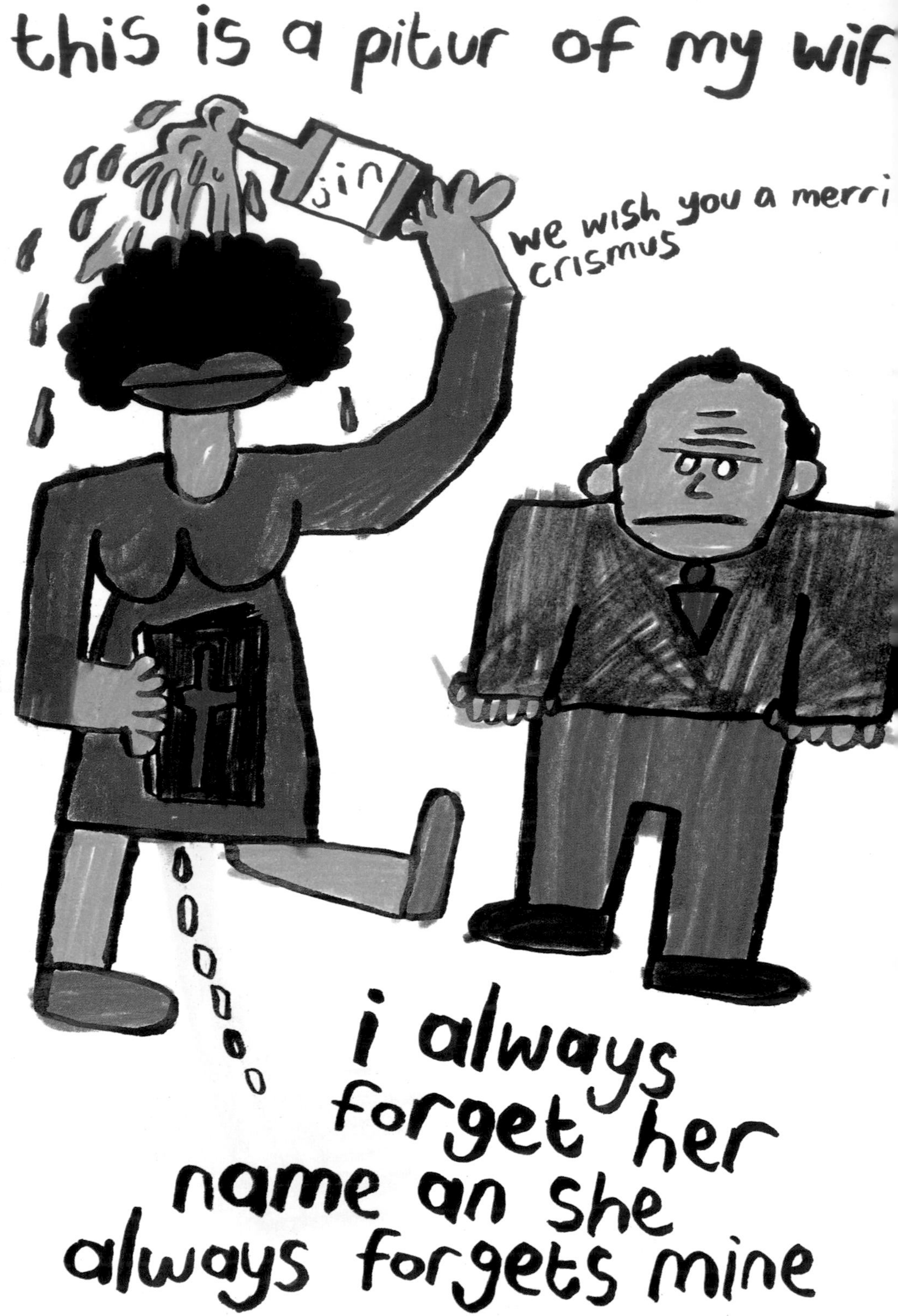
this is a pitur of my wif
jin
we wish you a merri crismus
i always forget her name an she always forgets mine

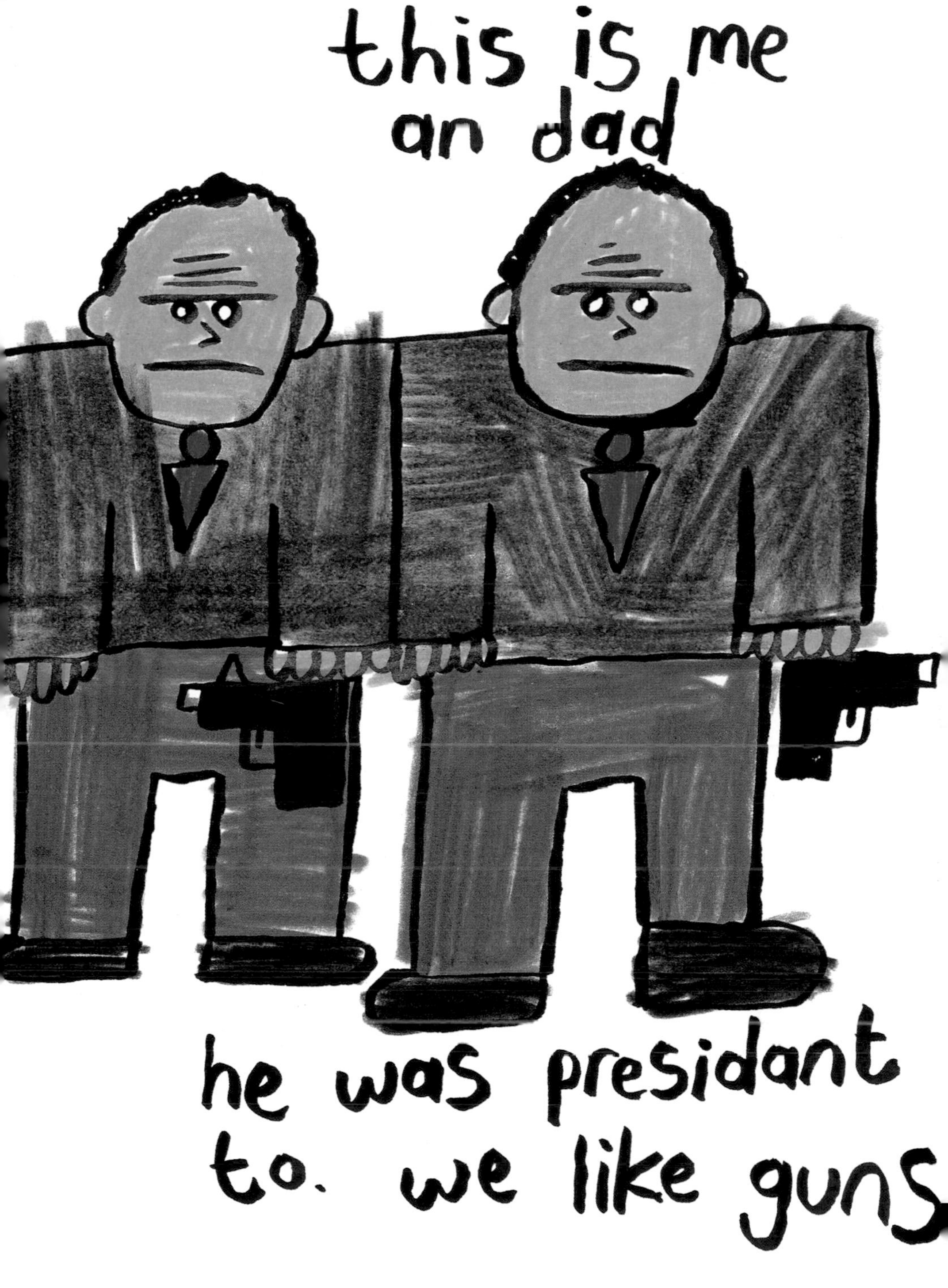
this is me
an dad
he was presidant
to. we like guns

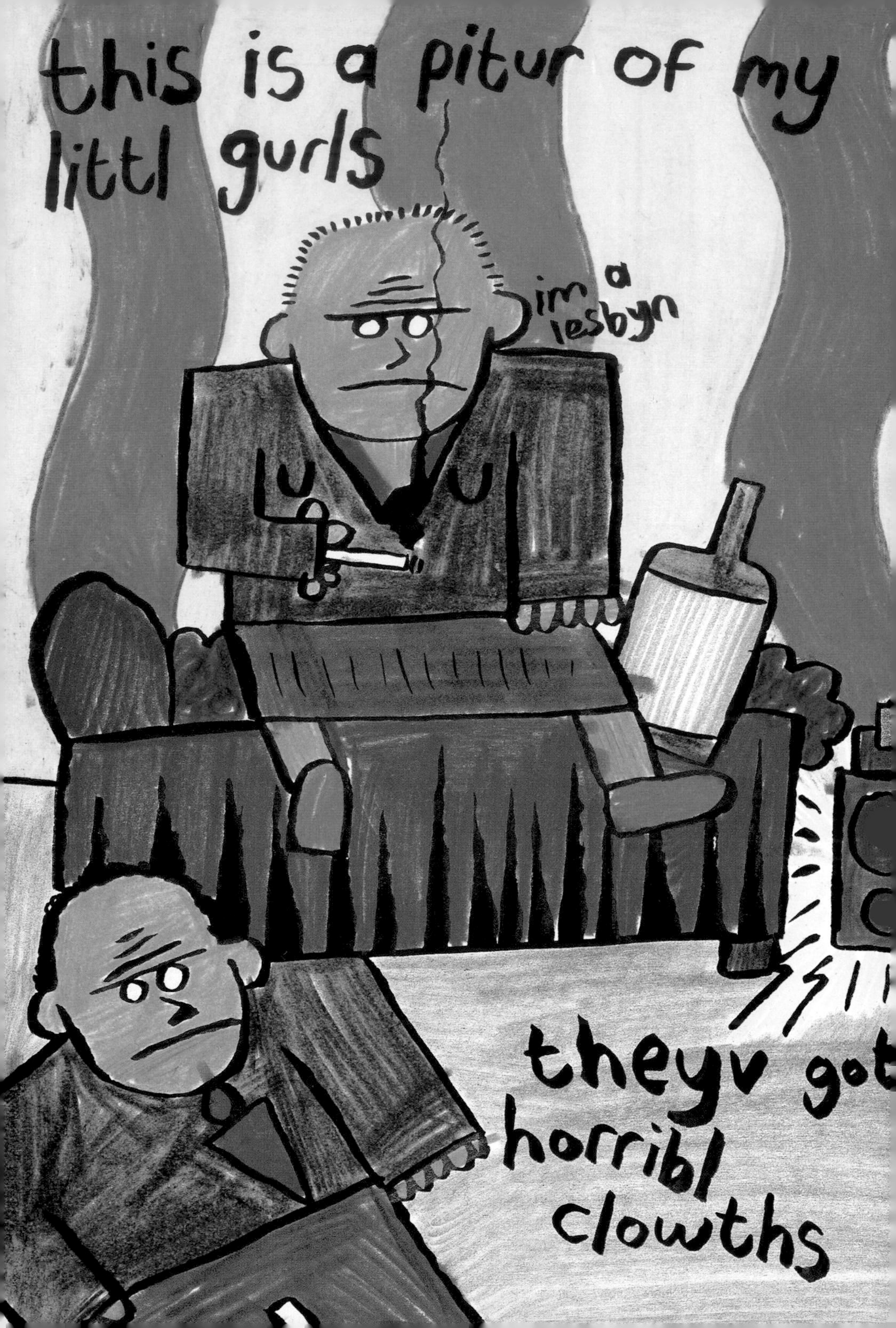
this is a pitur of my littl gurls
im a lesbyn
theyv got horribl clowths

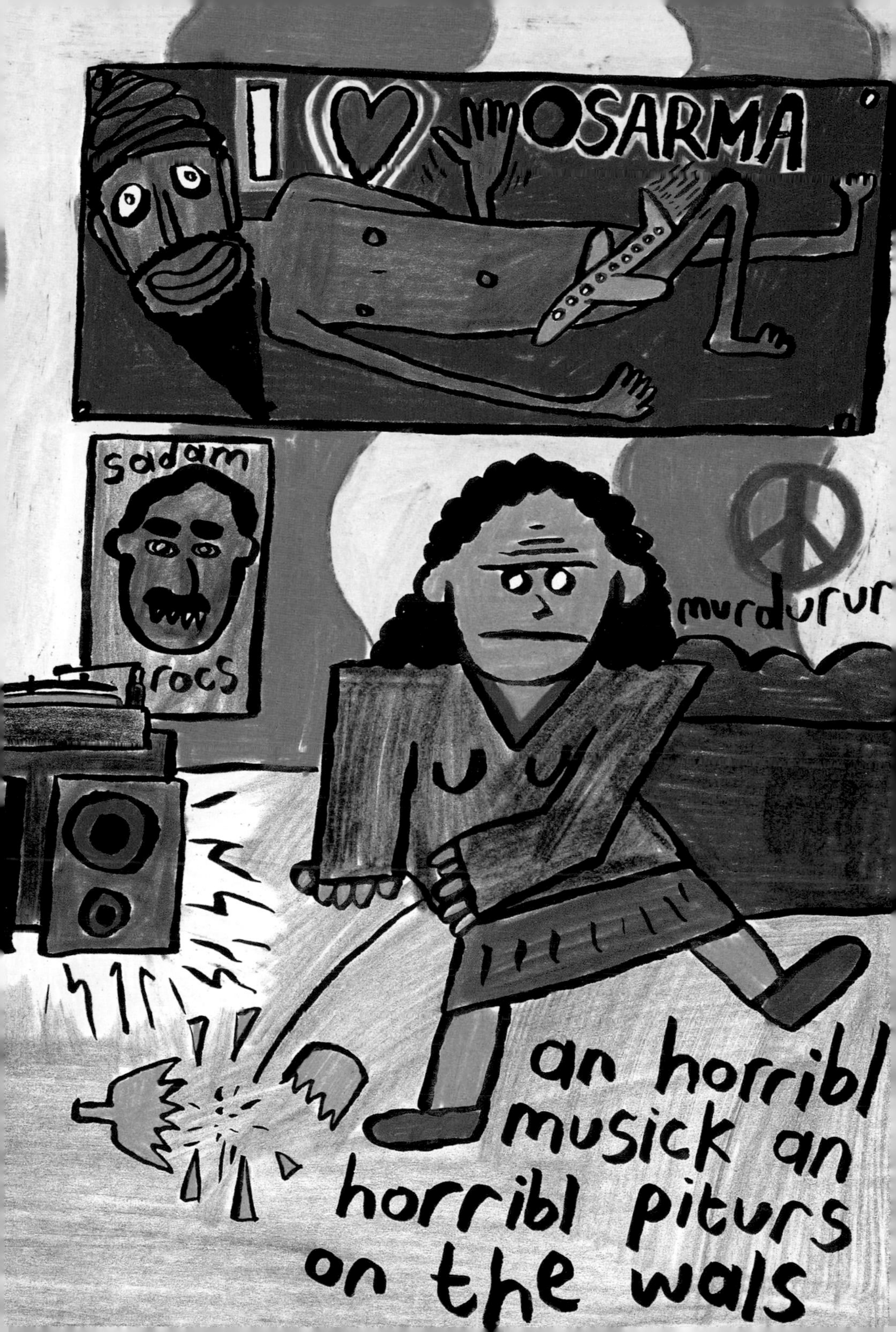
I ♥ OSARMA
sadam rocs
murdurur
an horribl musick an horribl piturs on the wals

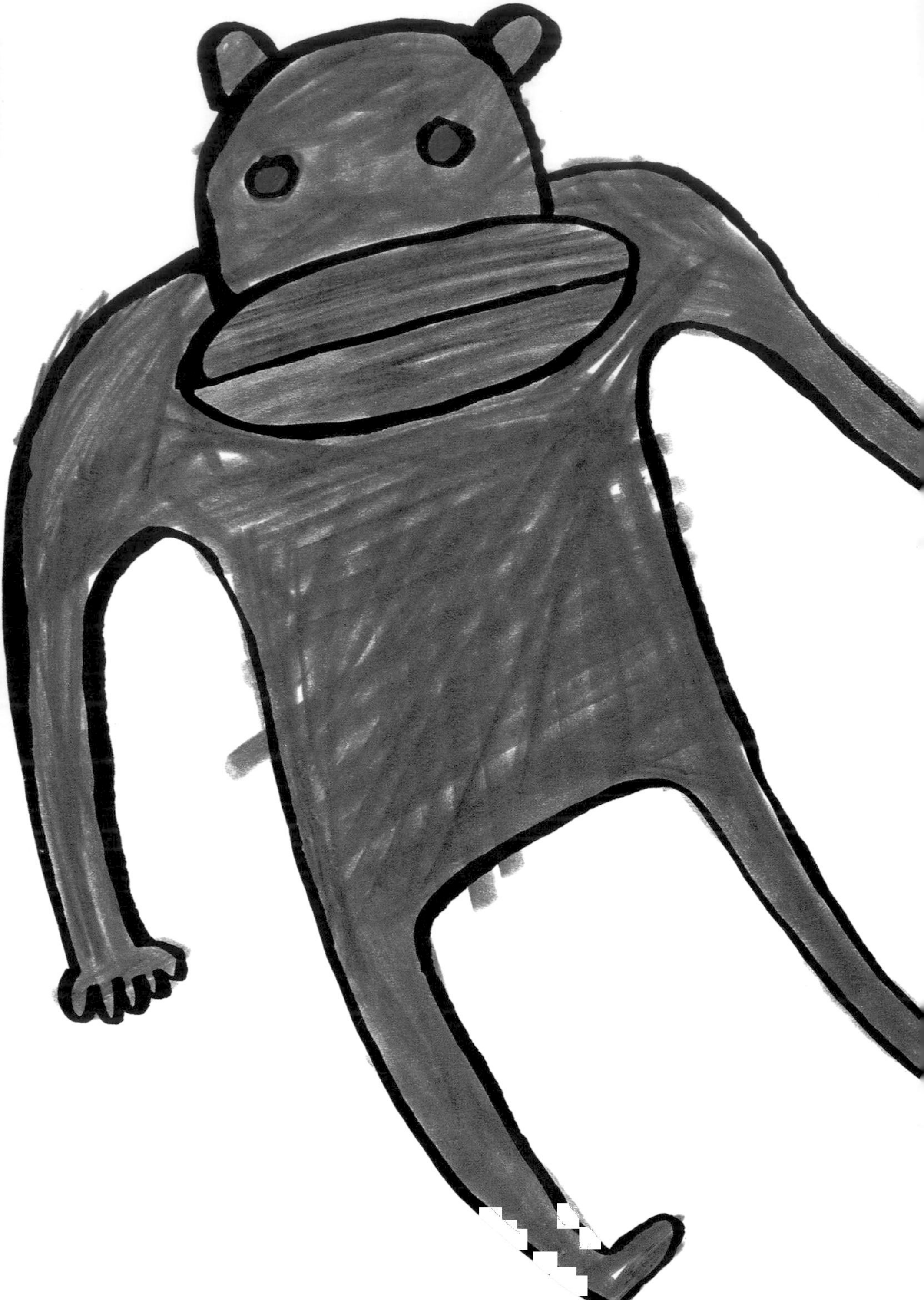

this is mr munky
i usd to talk to
him all the tiem

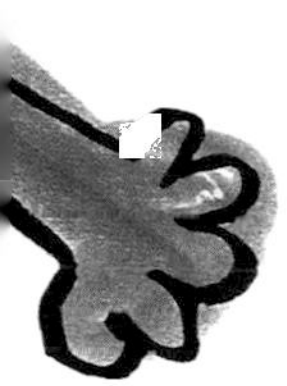

he was my best
frend

then i met tony

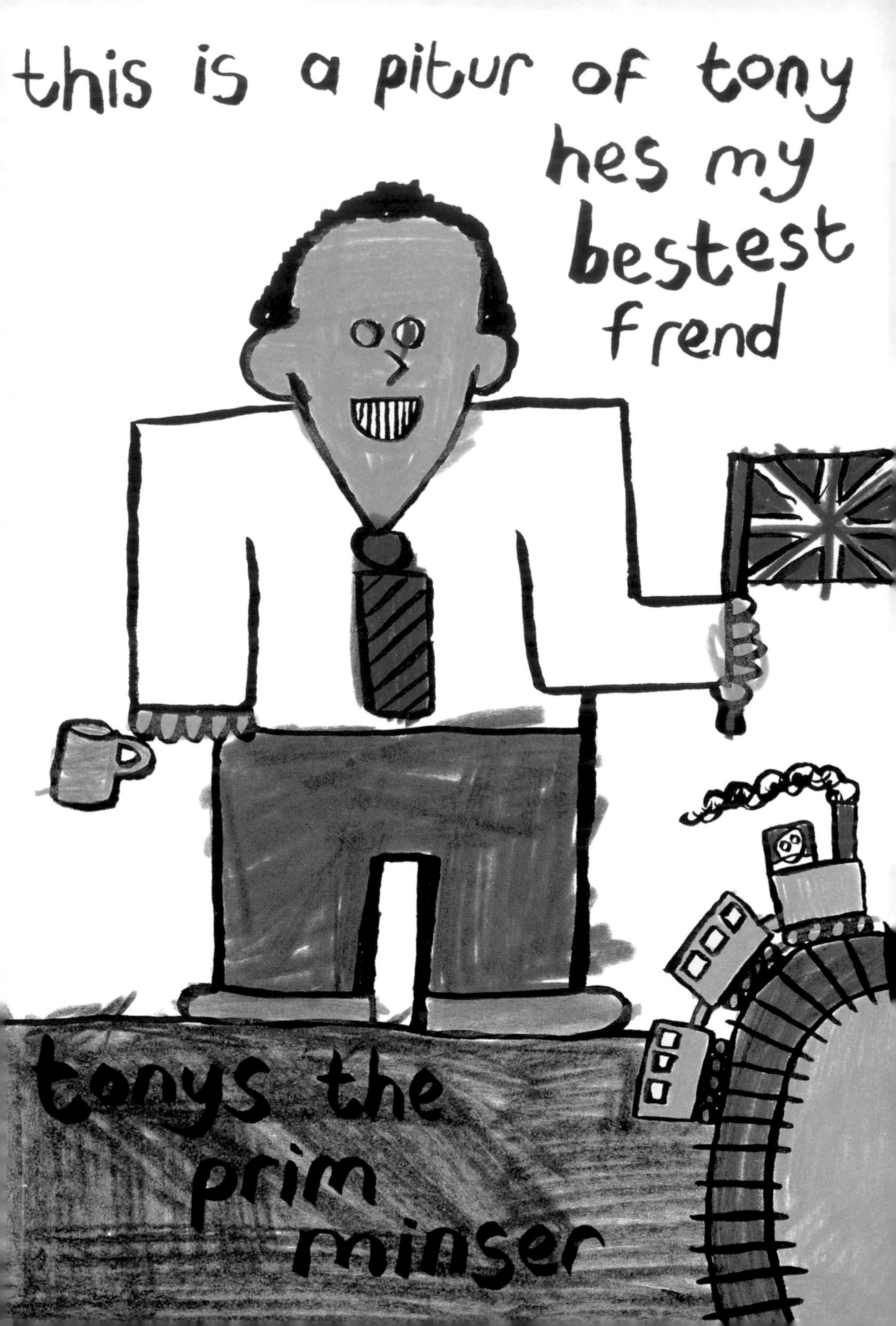
this is a pitur of tony
hes my bestest frend
tonys the prim minser

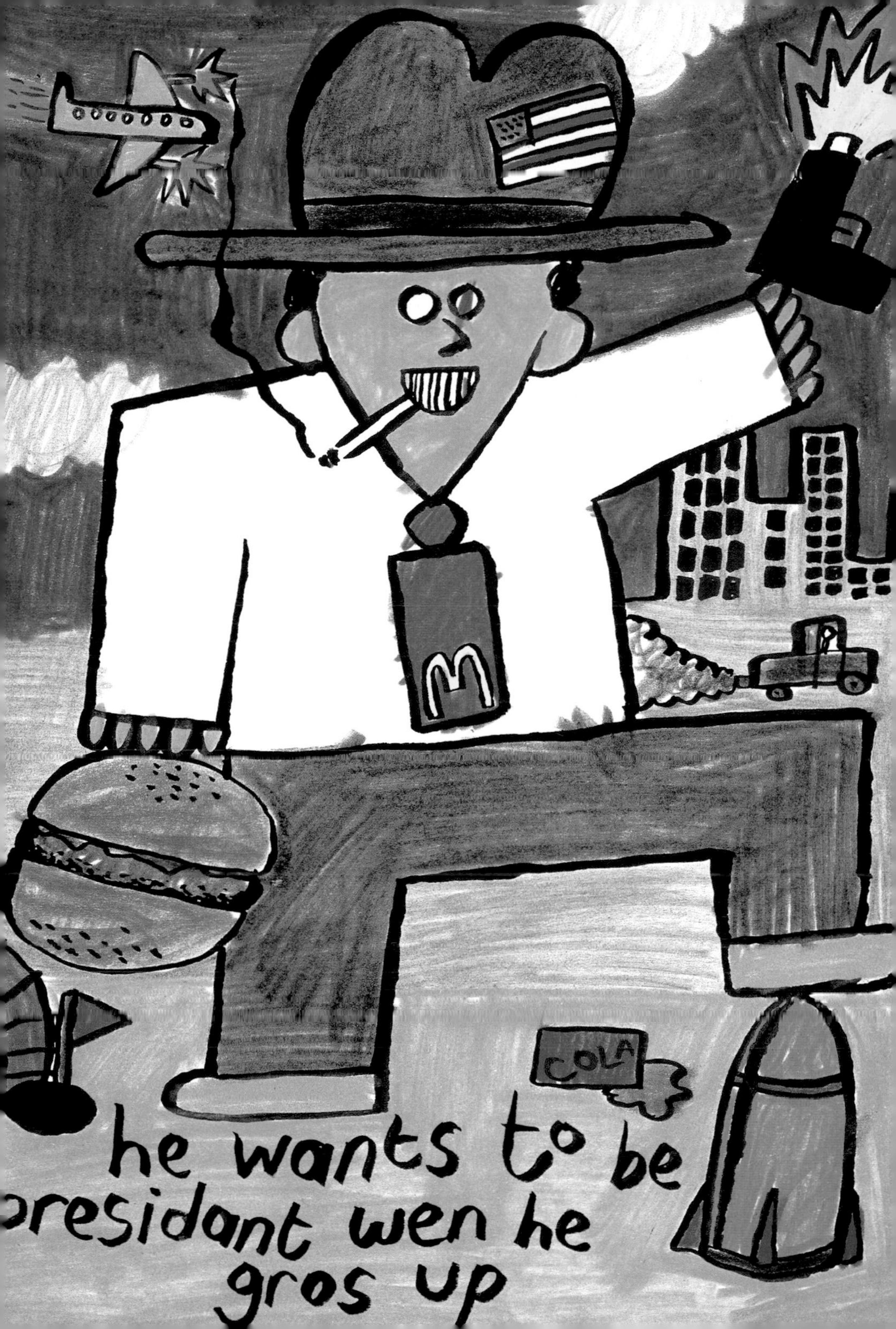
COLA
he wants to be
presidant wen he
gros up

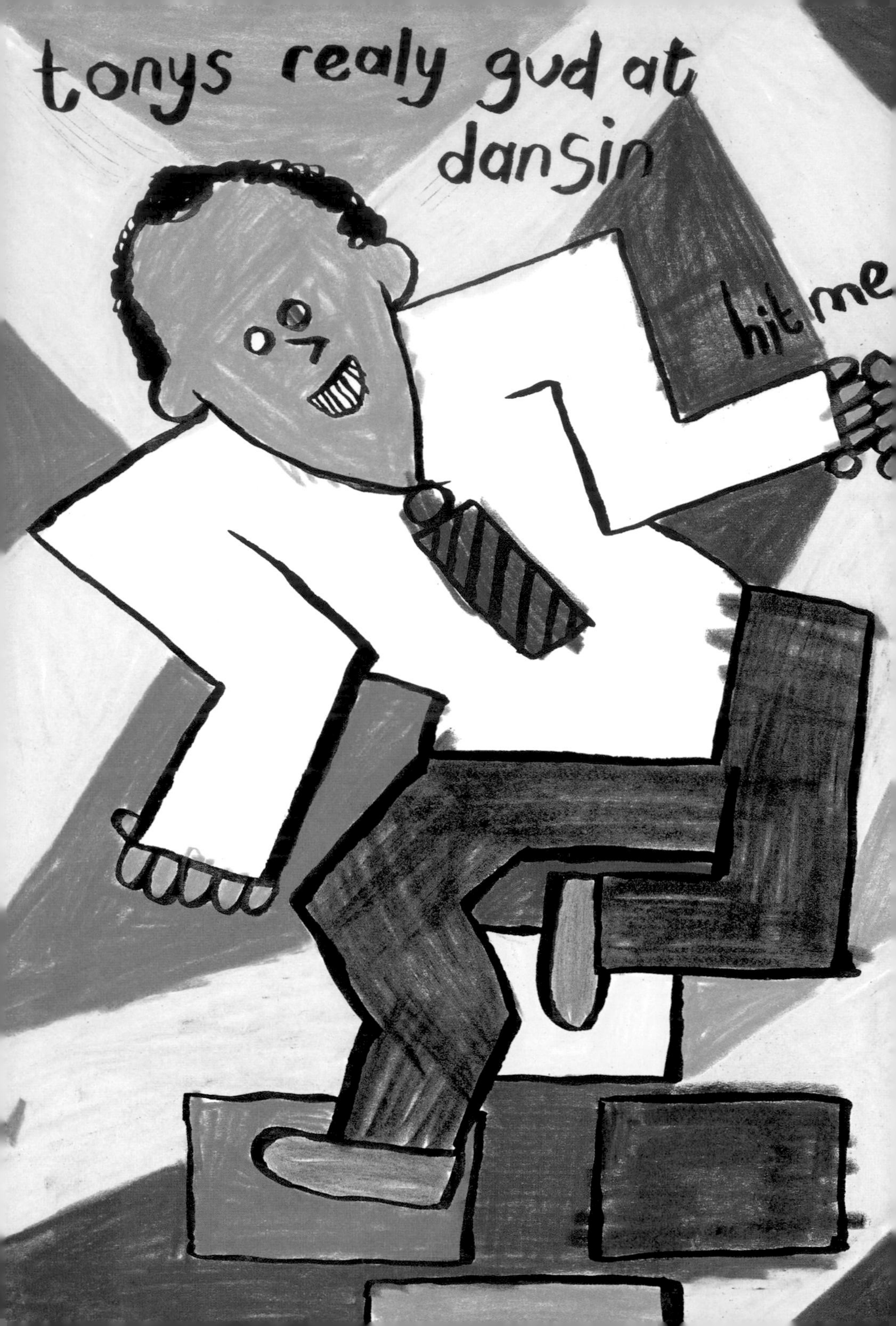
tonys realy gud at dansin
hit me

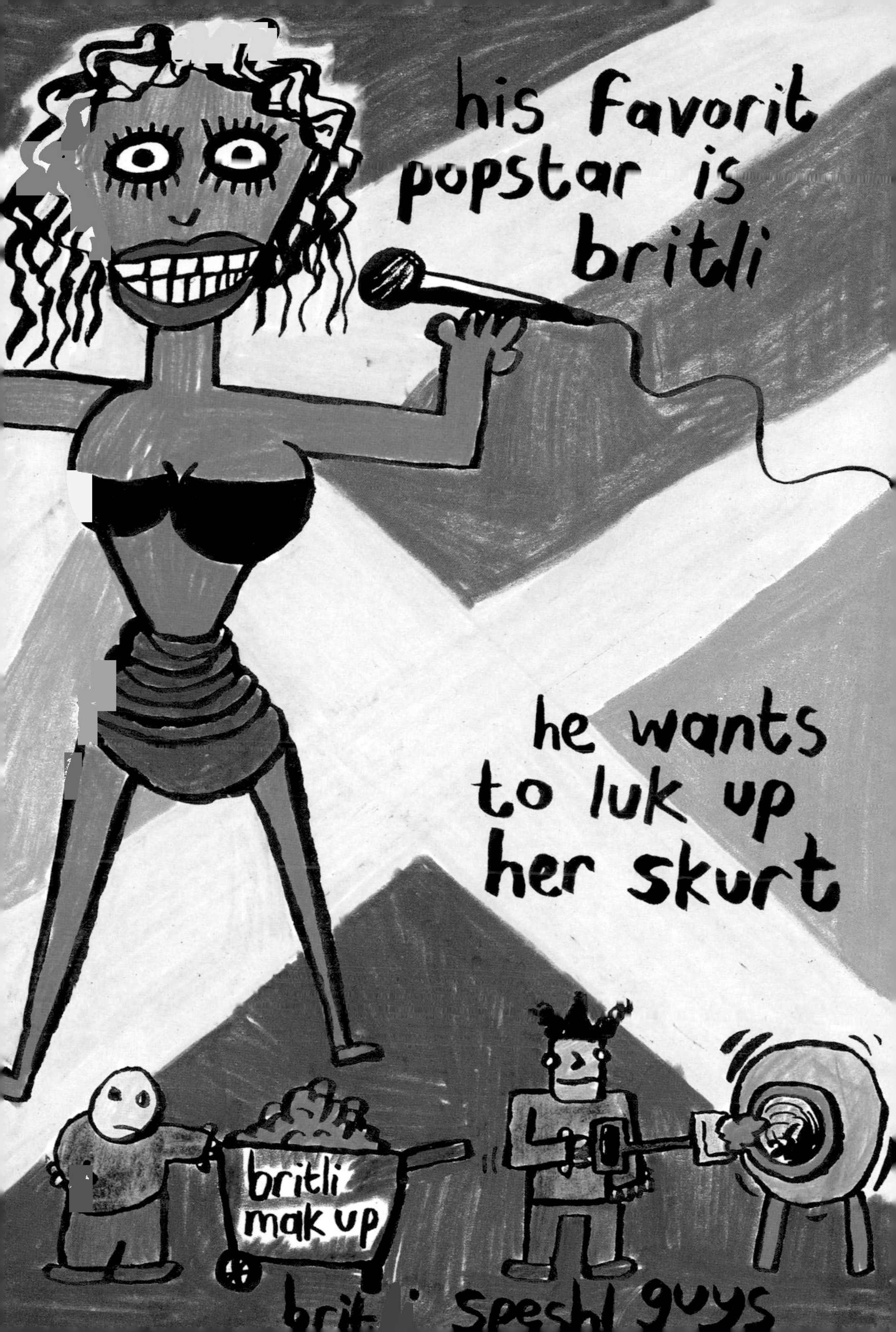
his favorit popstar is britli
he wants to luk up her skurt
britli mak up
brit i speshl guys

this is a pitur of cheri she was pretti wen he marid her but now shes realy ugly

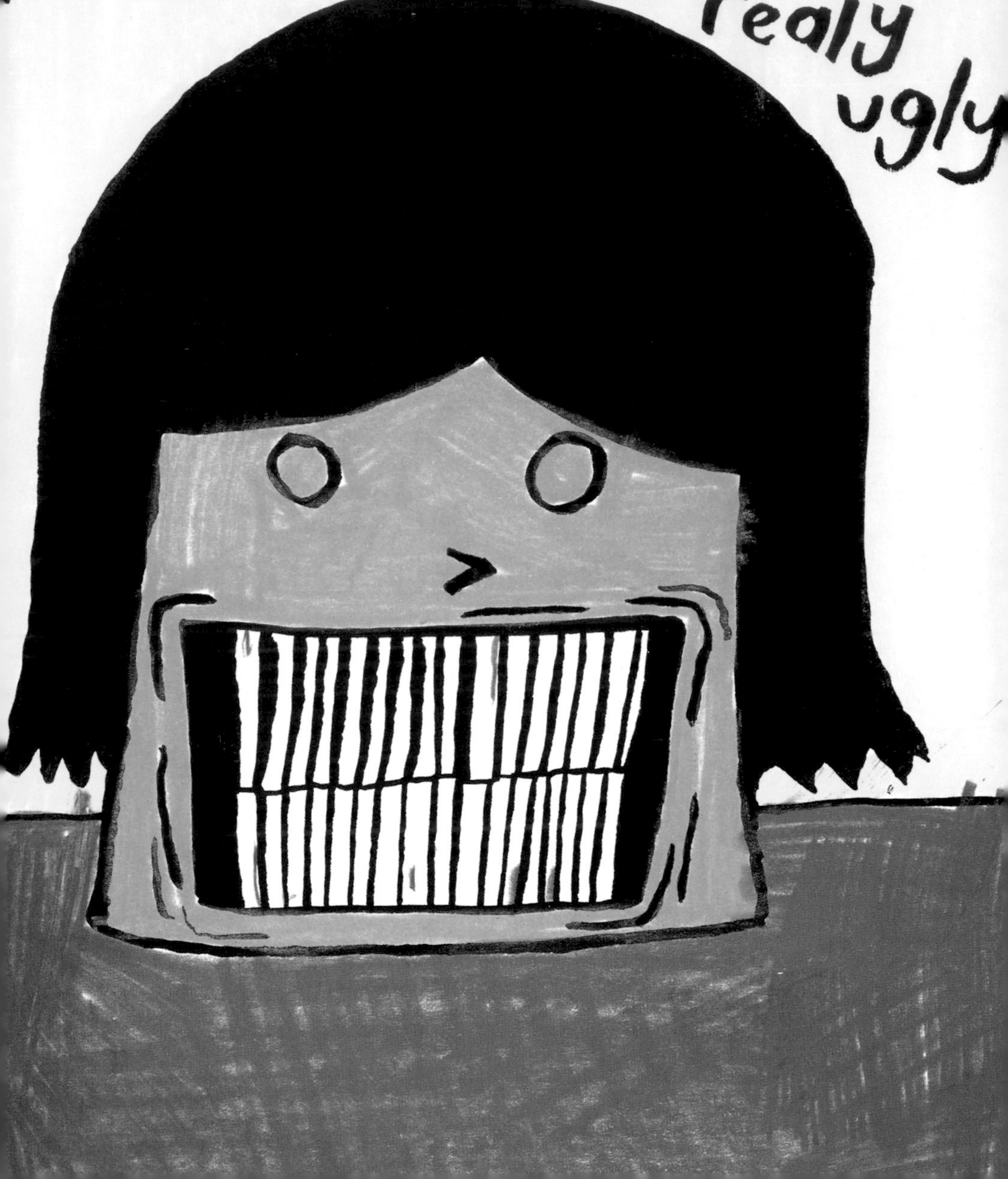

cheri can do
10000 pres
ups

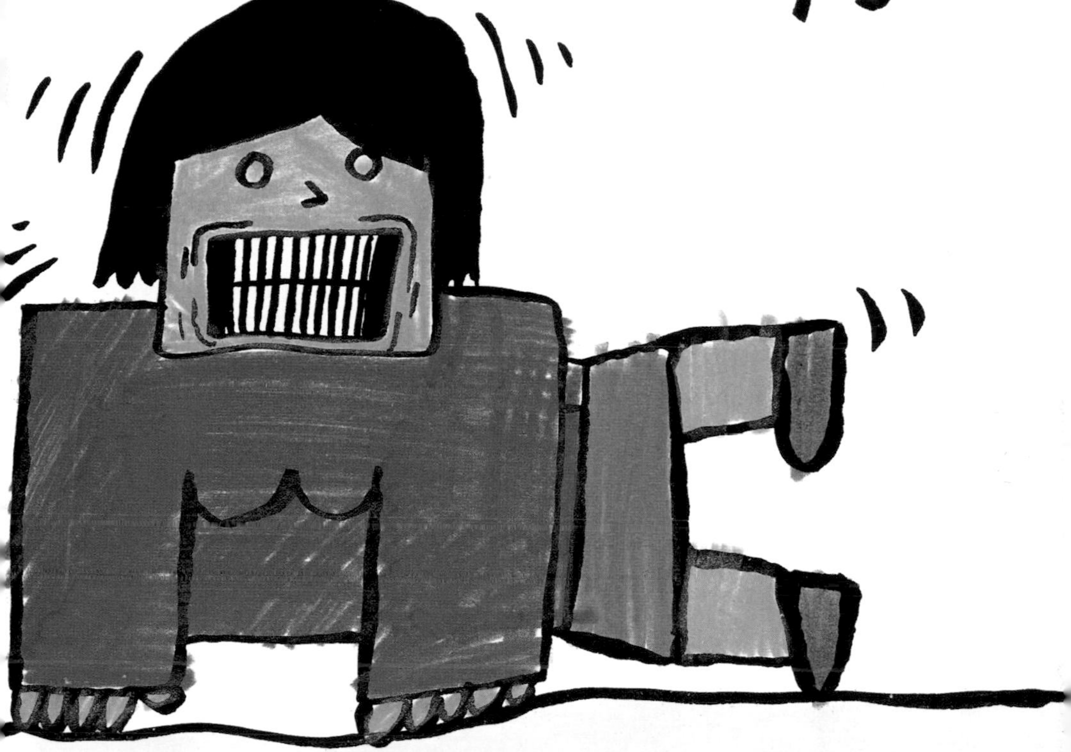

thats mor than me
an tony put togethr
i **hate** her

tony an cheri cum

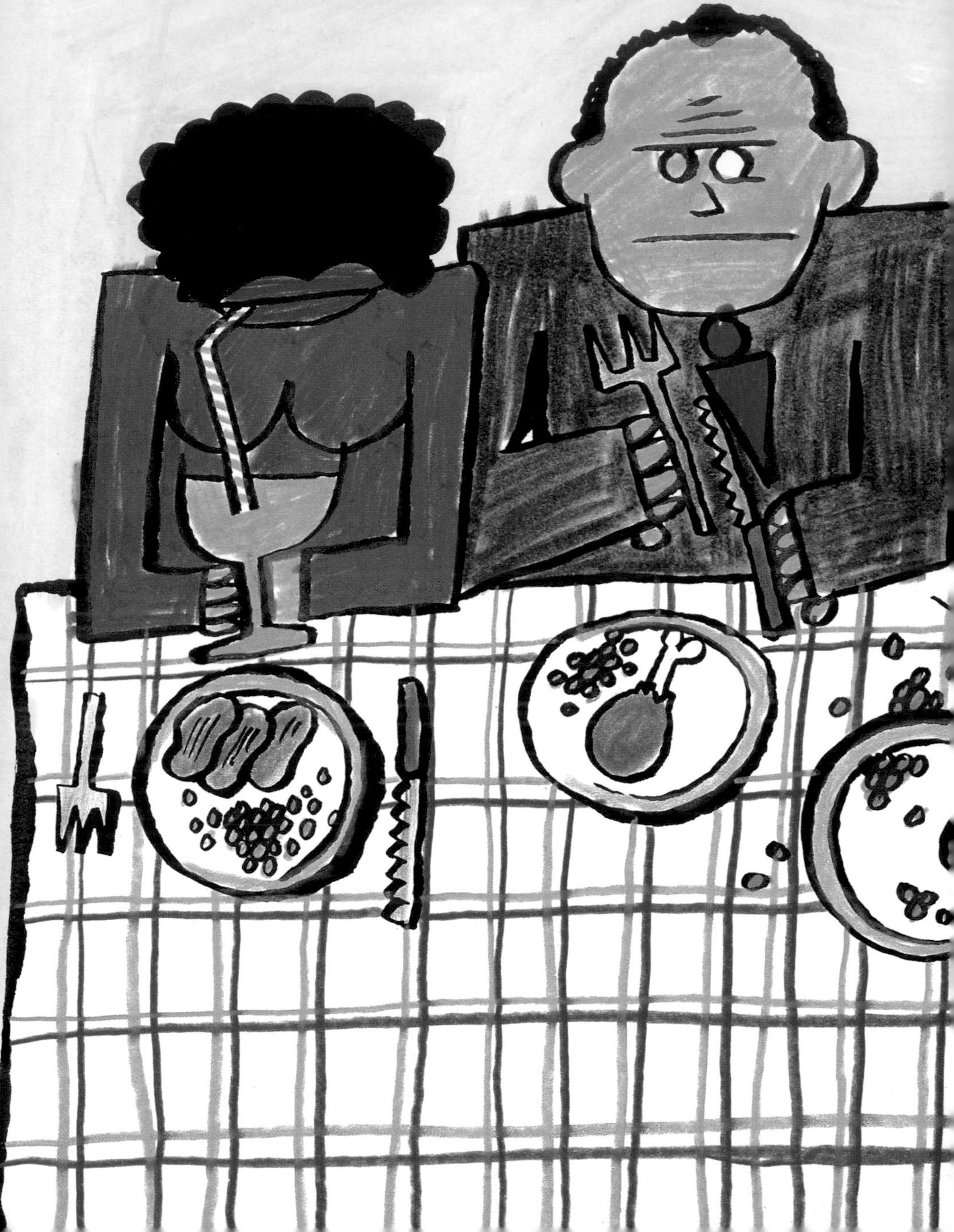

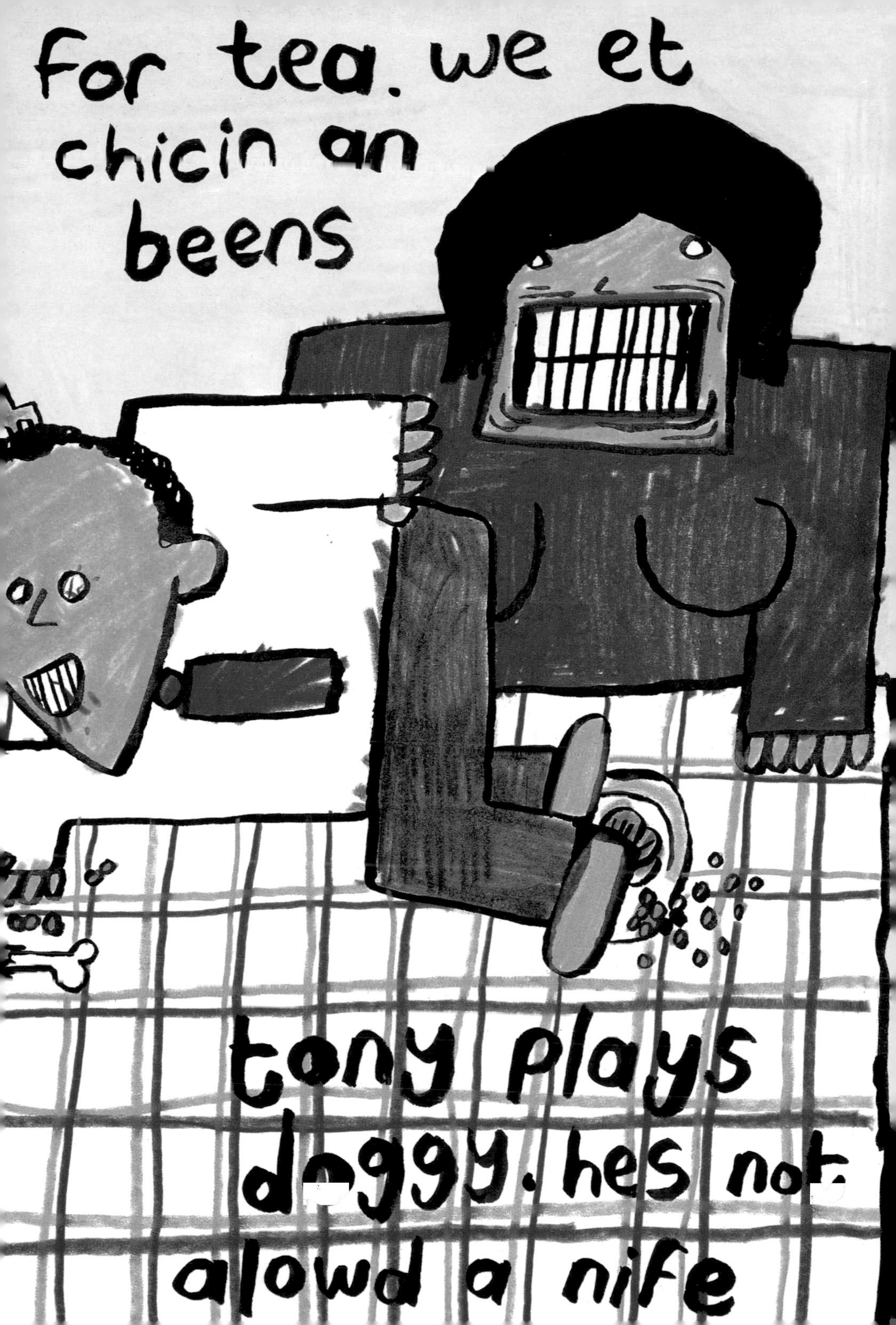
For tea. we et chicin an beens
tony plays doggy. hes not alowd a nife

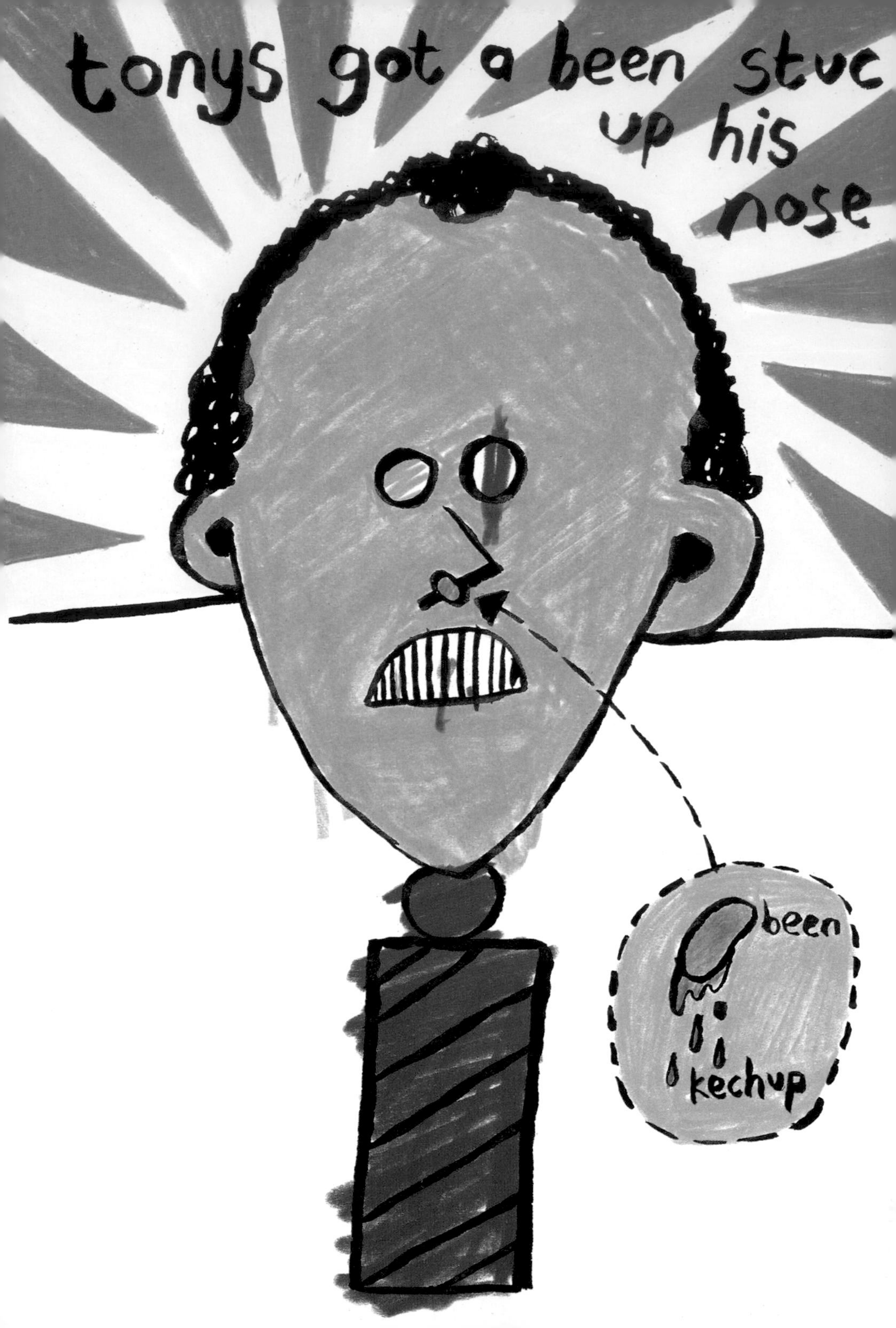
tonys got a been stuc up his nose
been
kechup

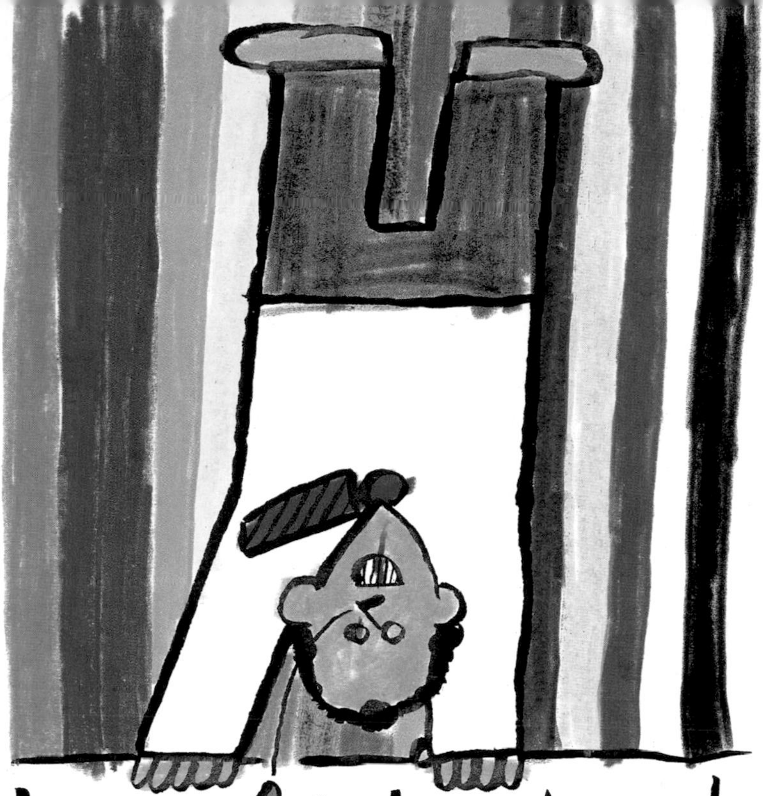

he hád to stand upsiyd down to get it out

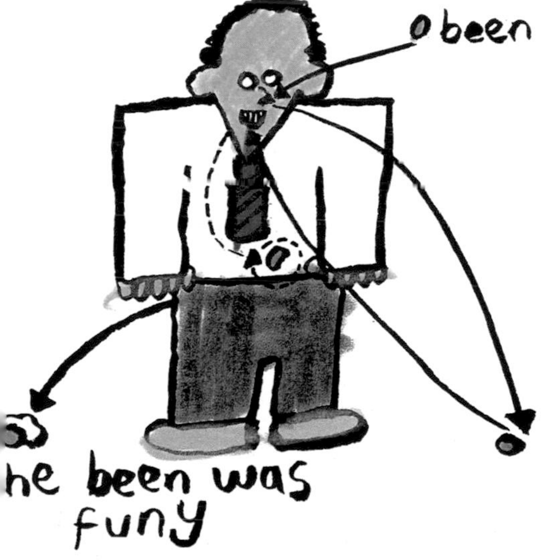
been
he been was funy

then he et it

yuc!

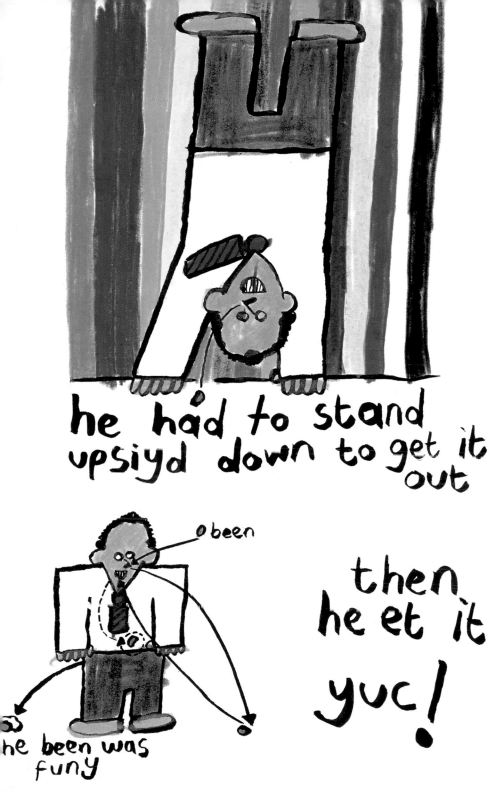

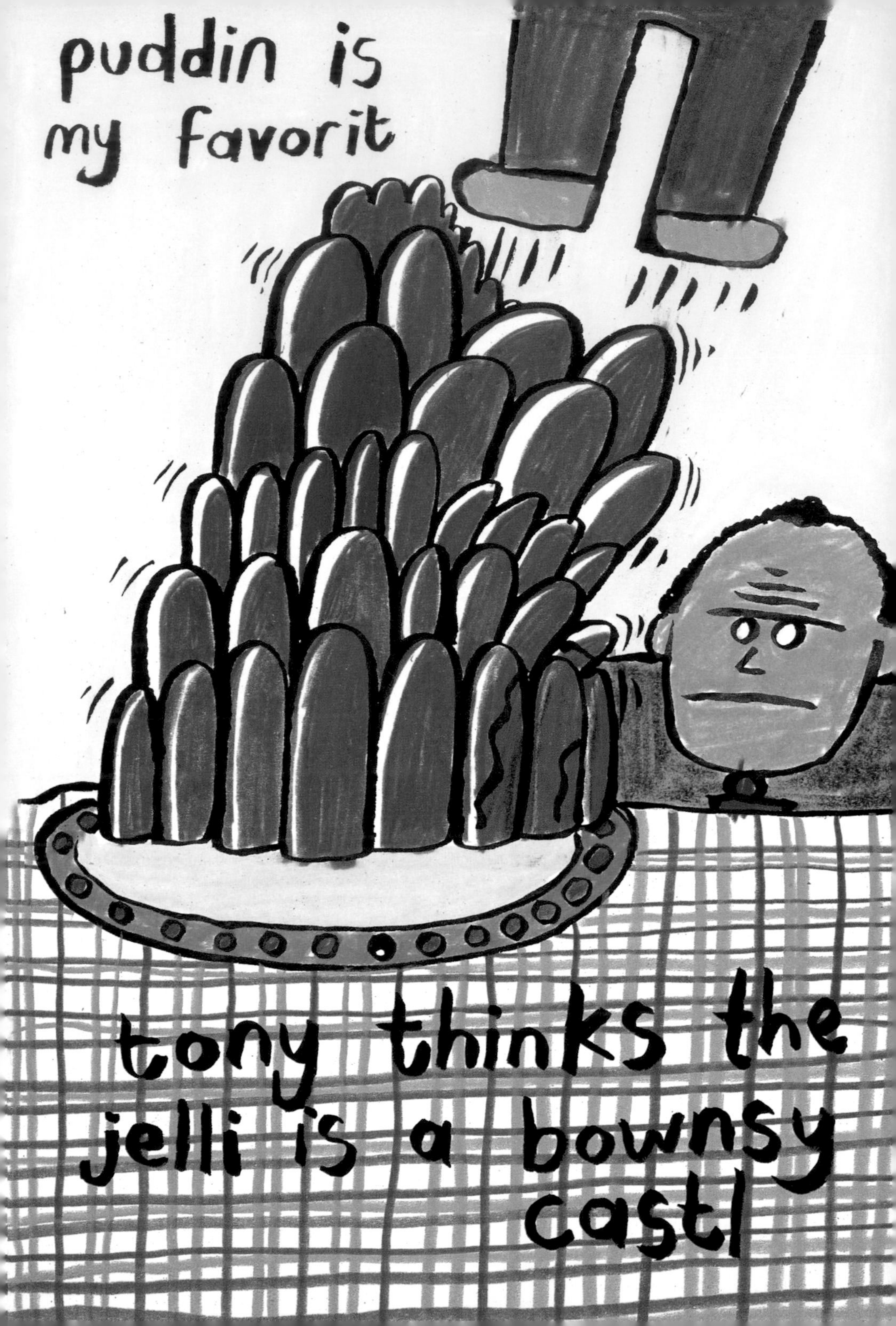
puddin is my favorit
tony thinks the jelli is a bownsy castl

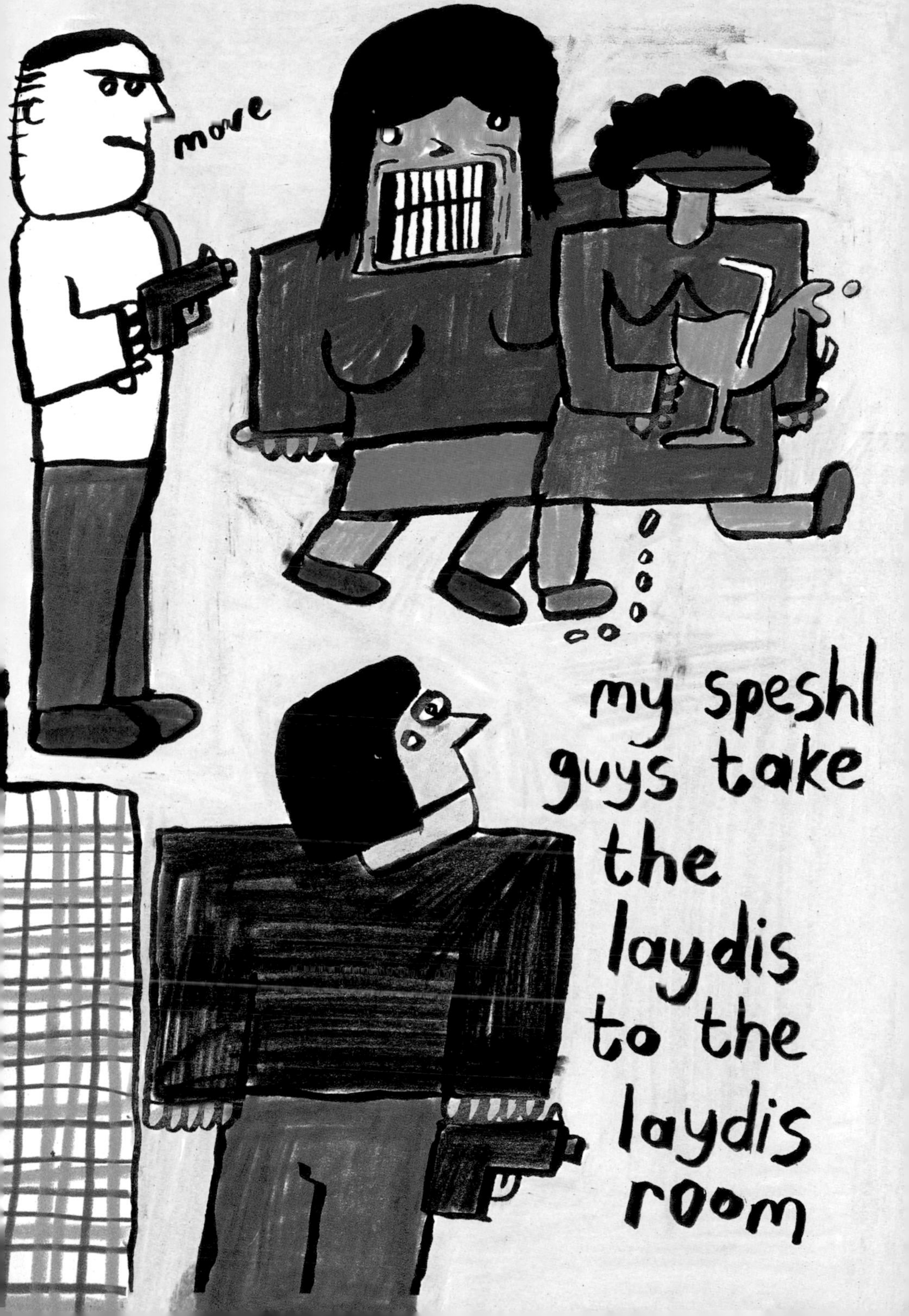
move
my speshl guys take the laydis to the laydis room

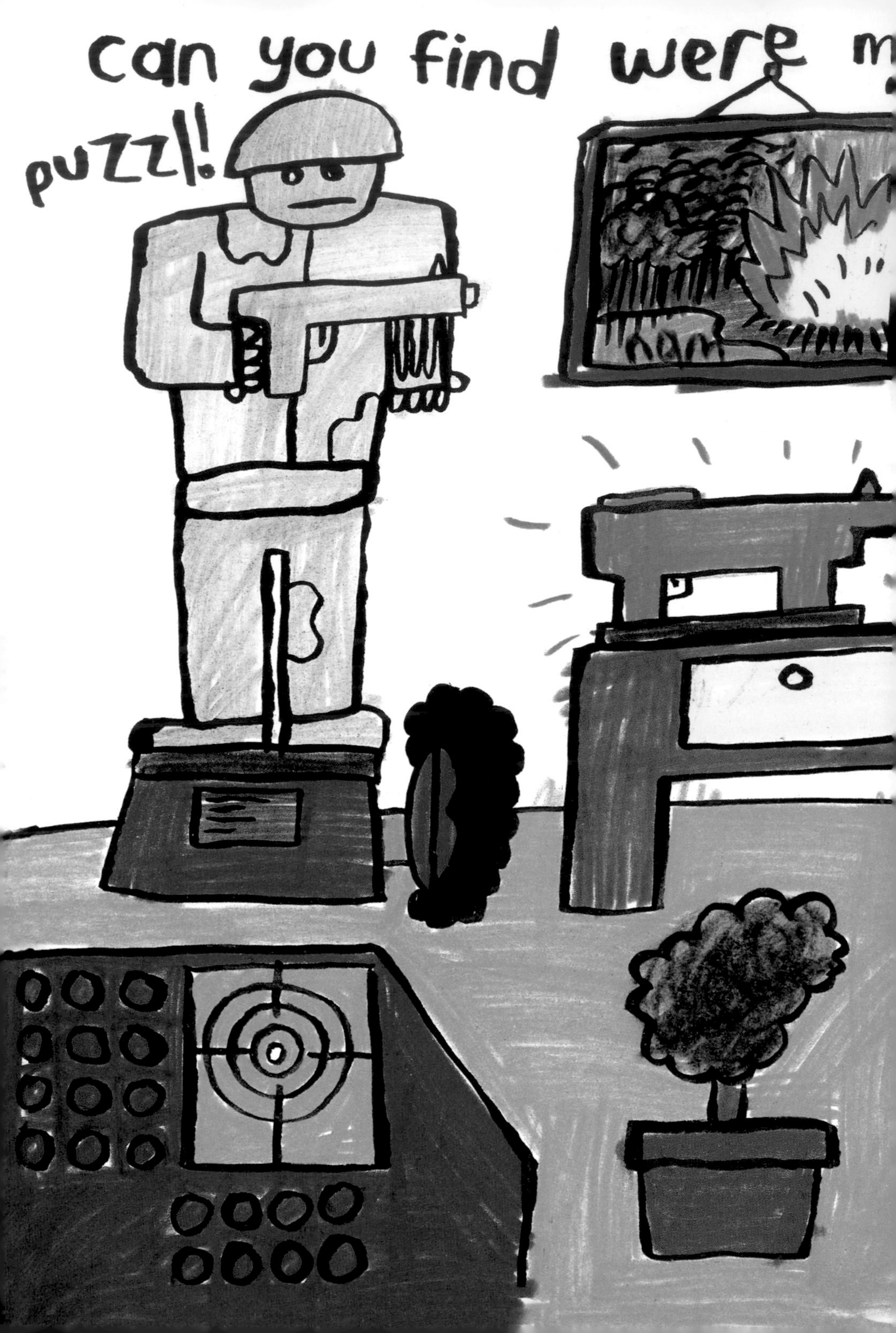
can you find were m
puzzl!

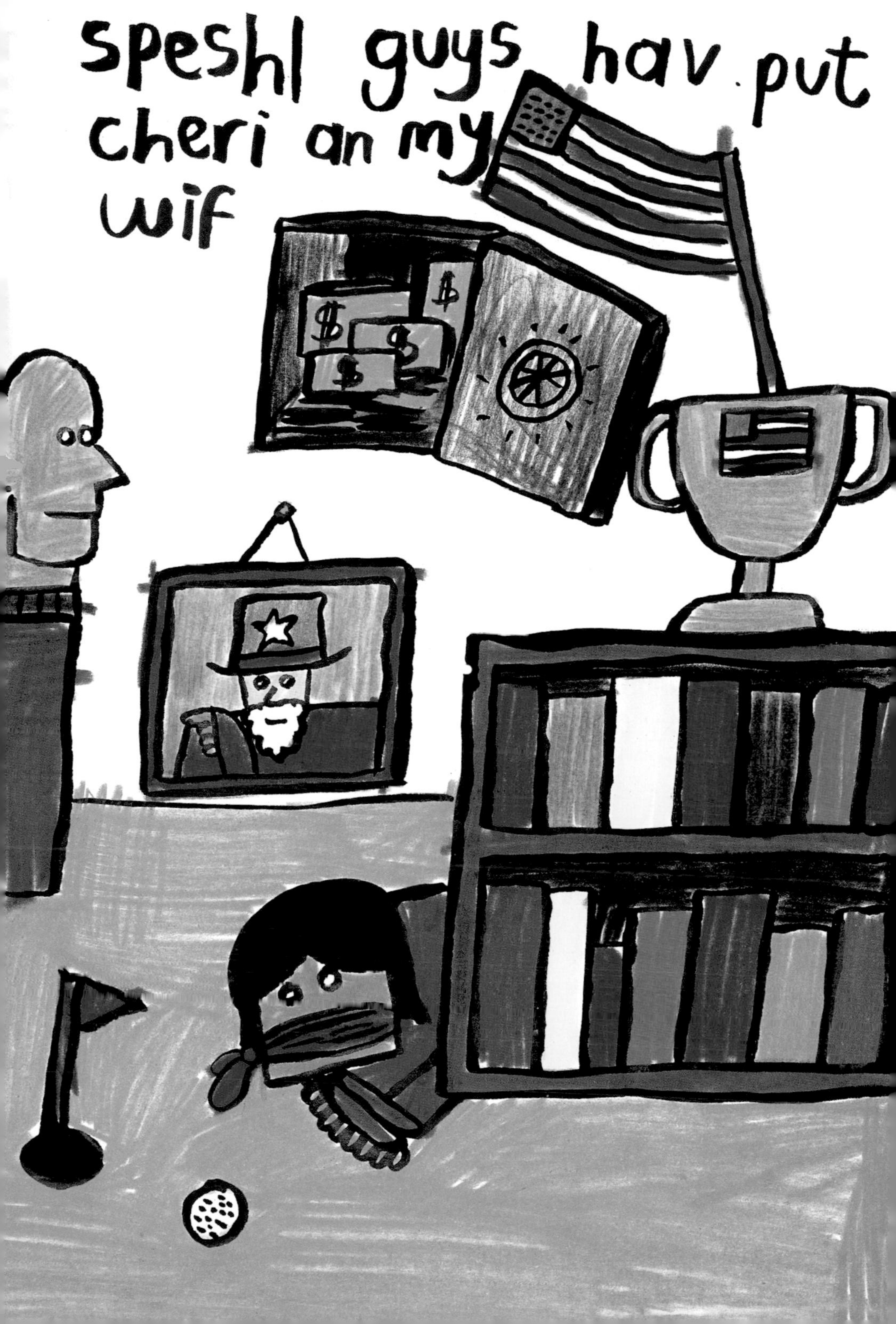
speshl guys hav put cheri an my wif

me an tony play
doctors an nurss

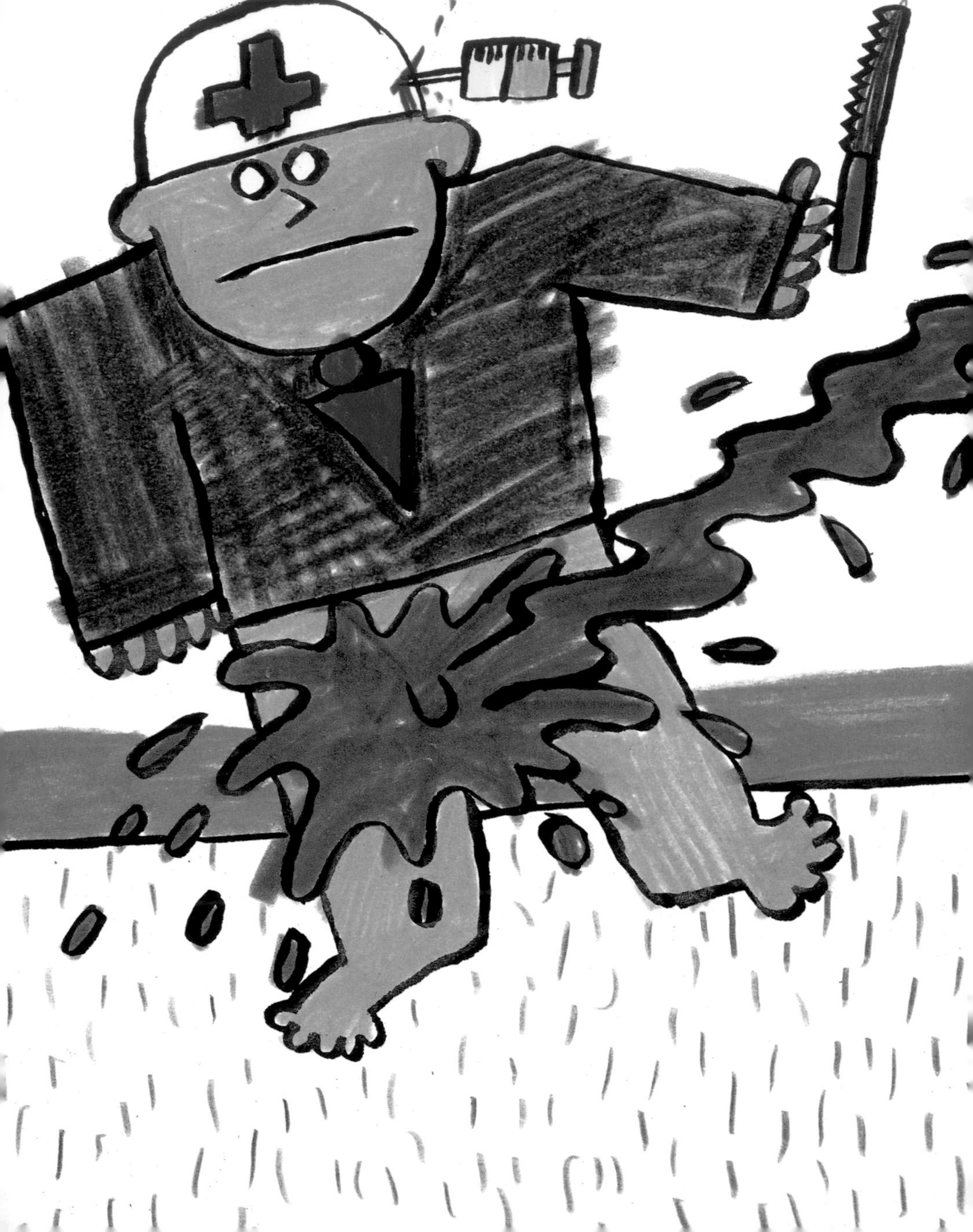

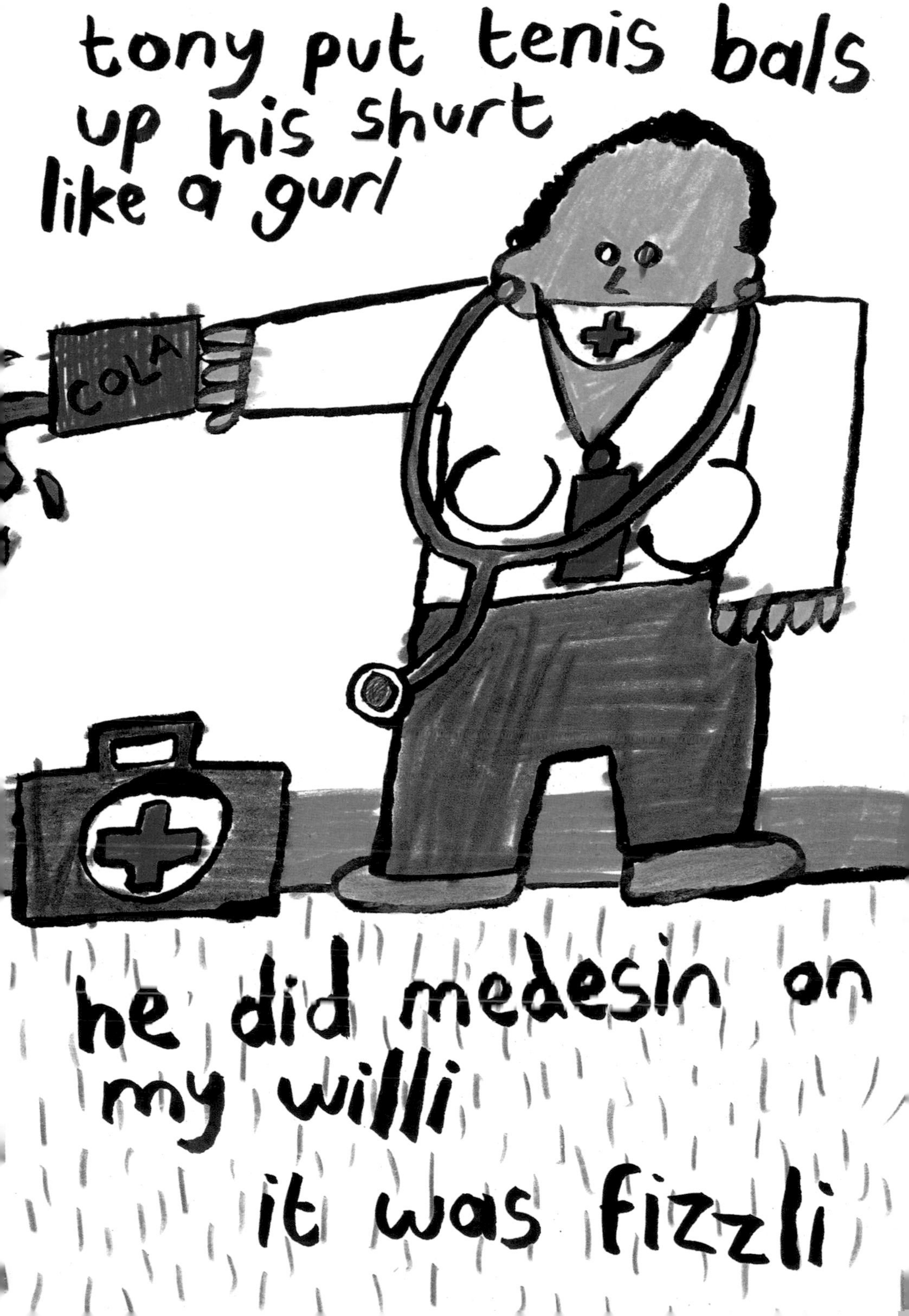
tony put tenis bals up his shurt like a gurl
COLA
he did medesin on my willi
it was fizzli

we play hide an seek

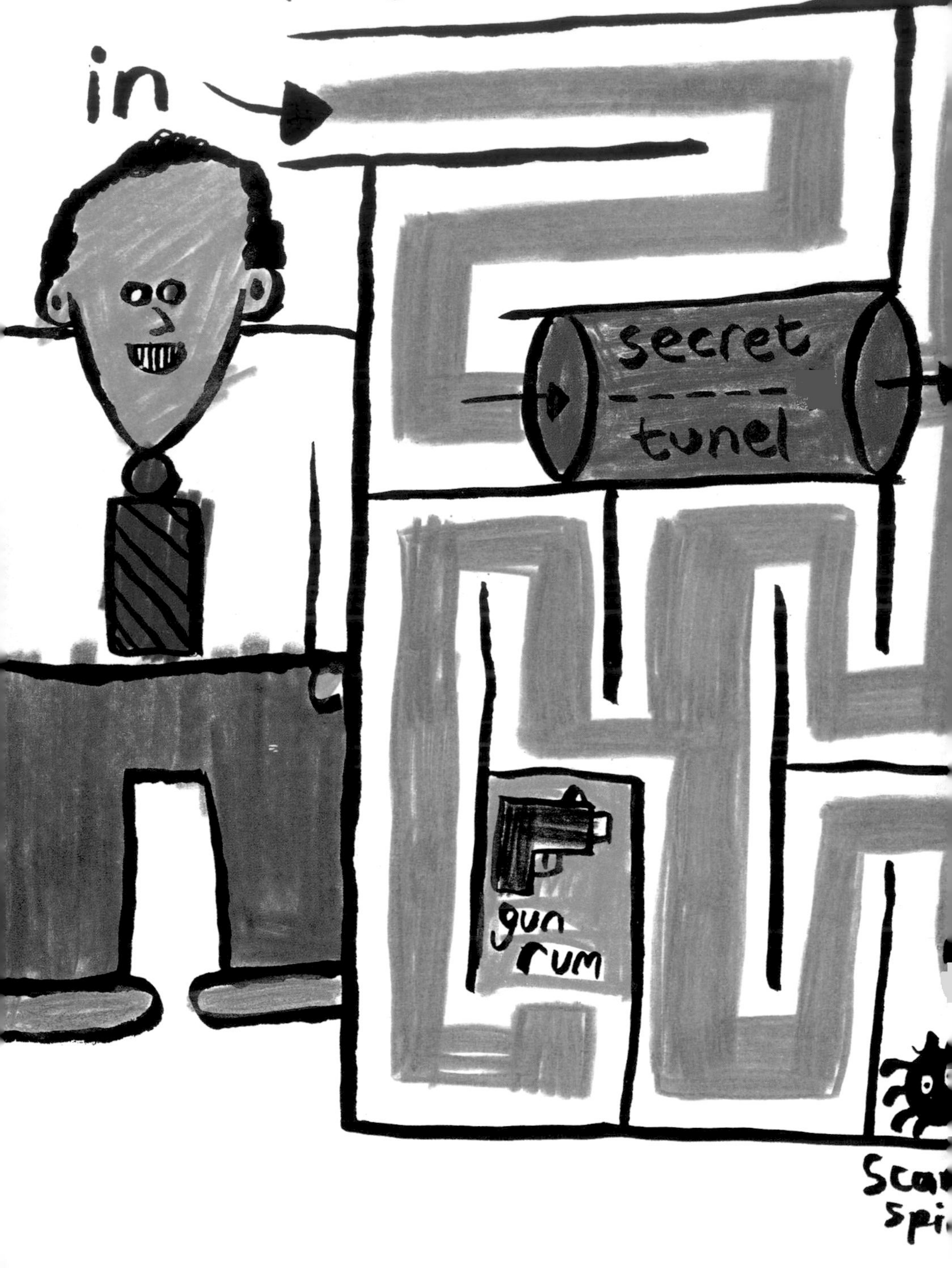

in
secret tunel
gun rum

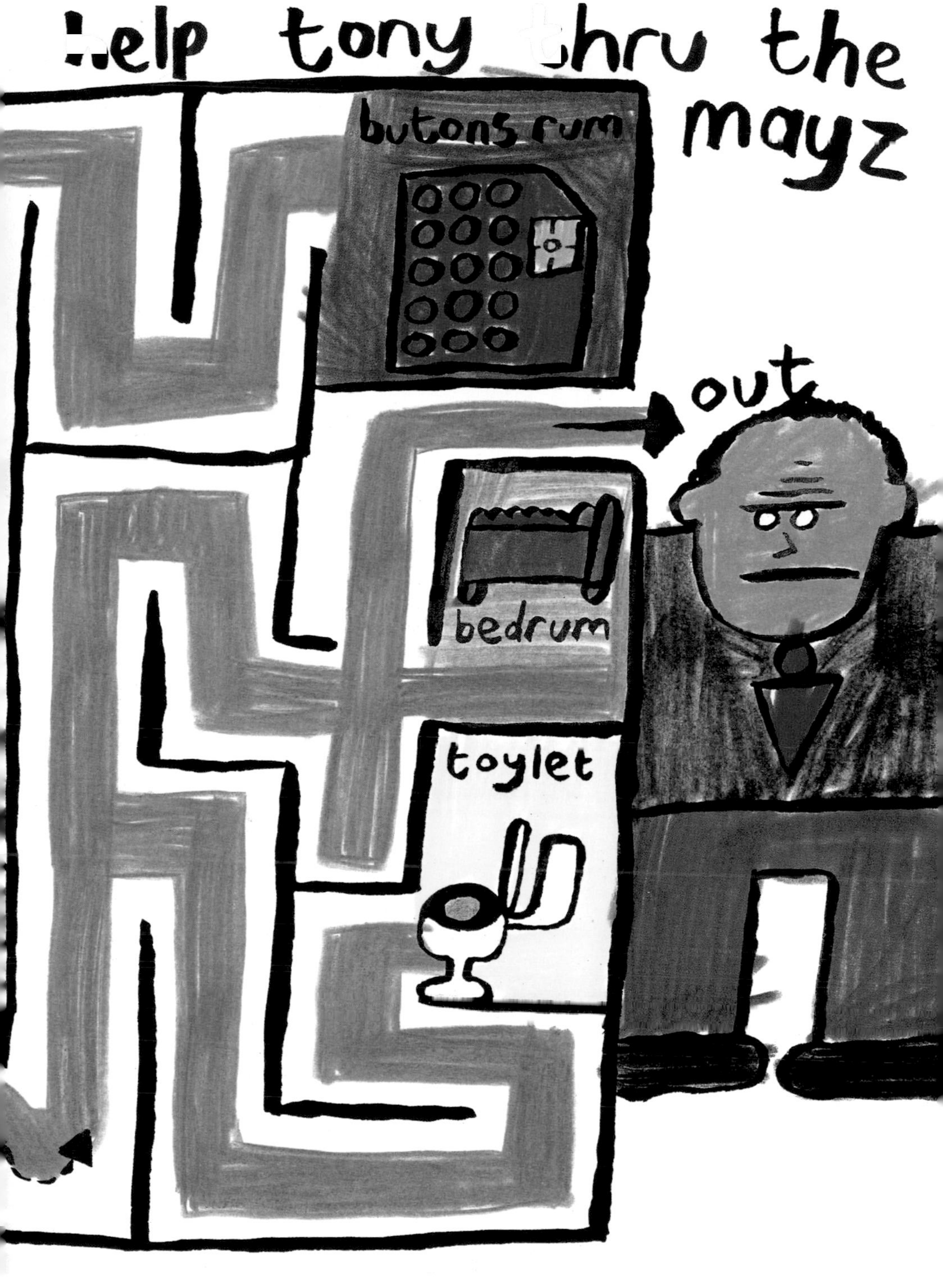
help tony thru the mayz
butons rum
out
bedrum
toylet

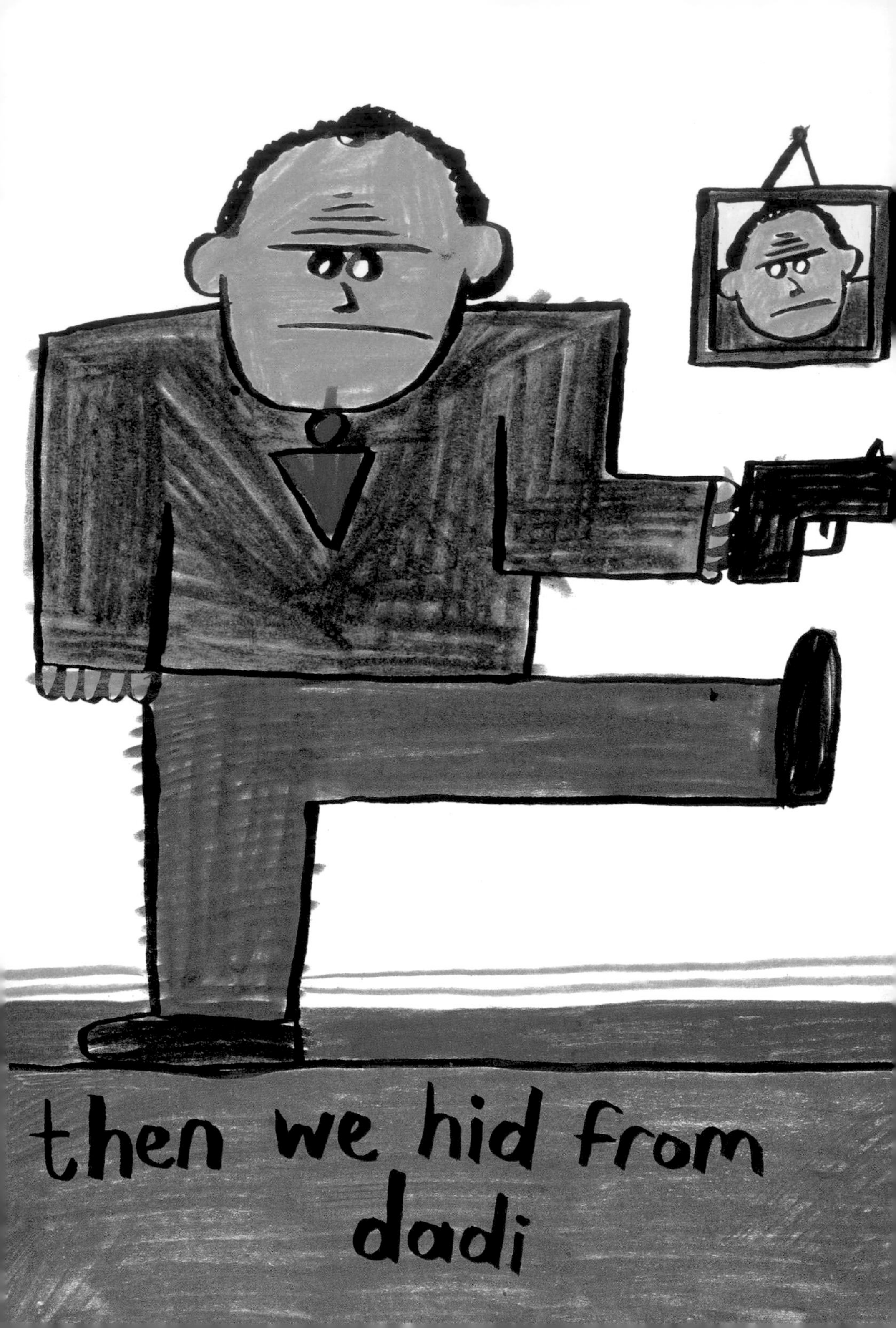
then we hid from
dadi

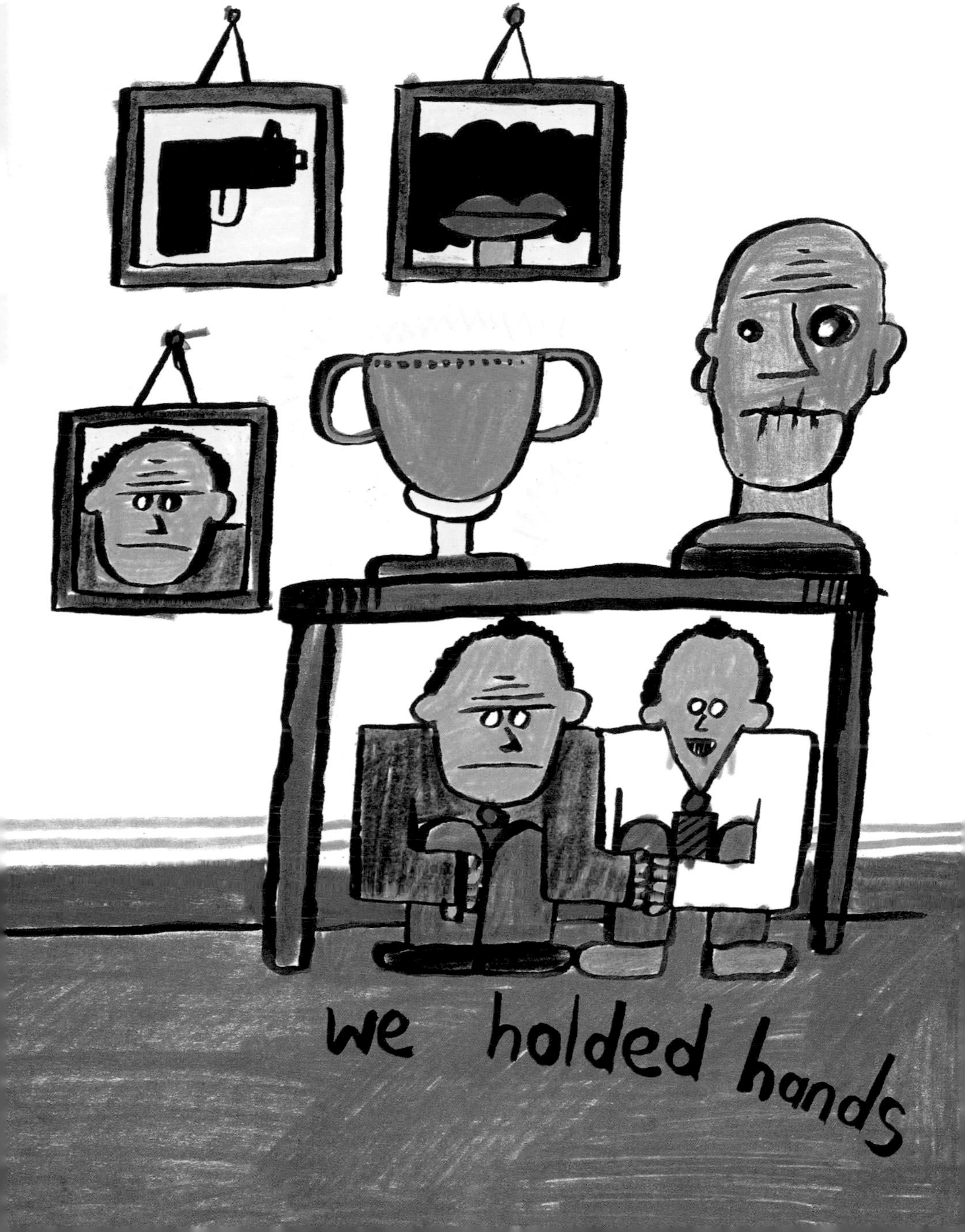
we holded hands

me an tony draw piturs

tony drawd this

i drawd this

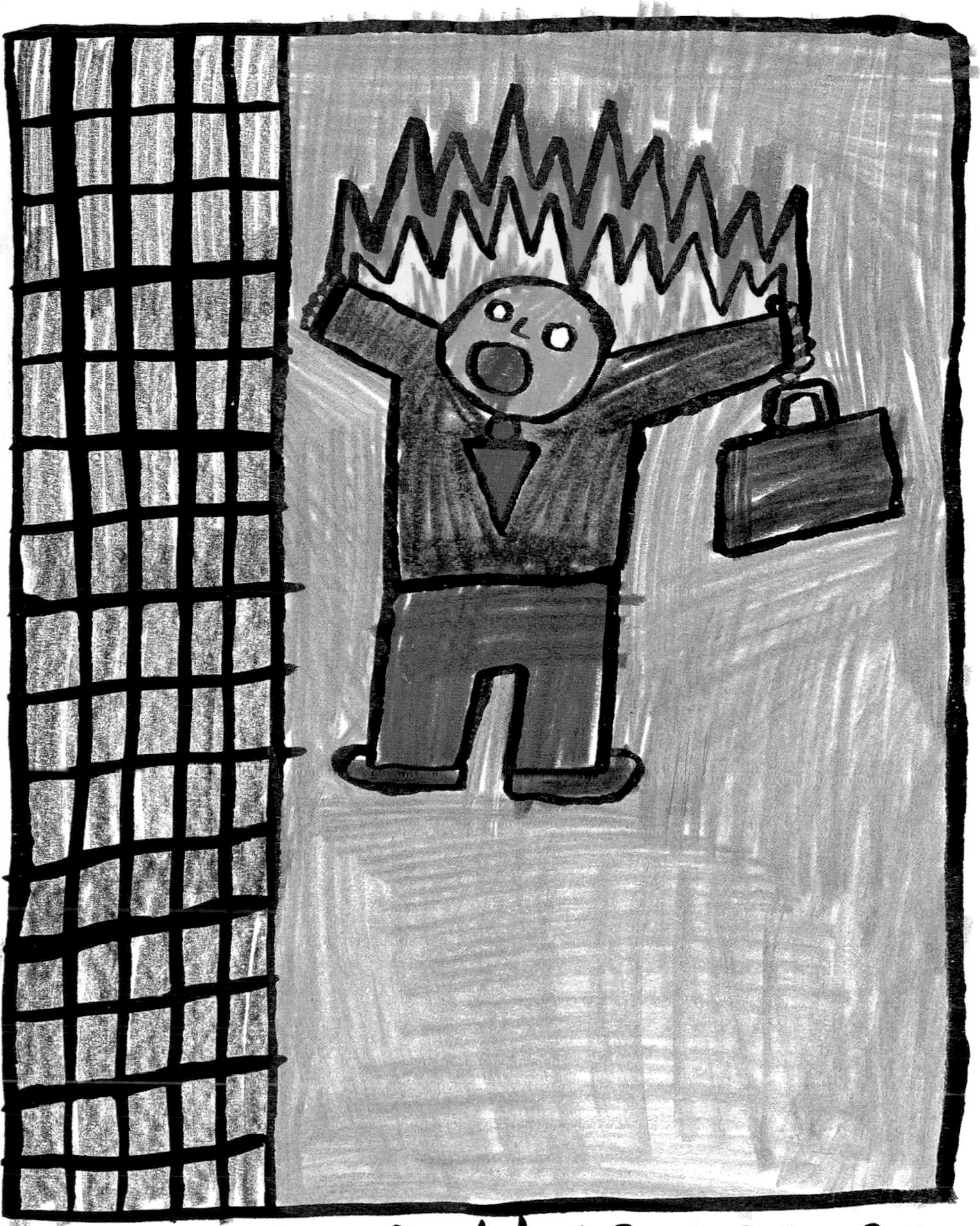

tony says ther are no ded americuns. only ded americun heros. i like that

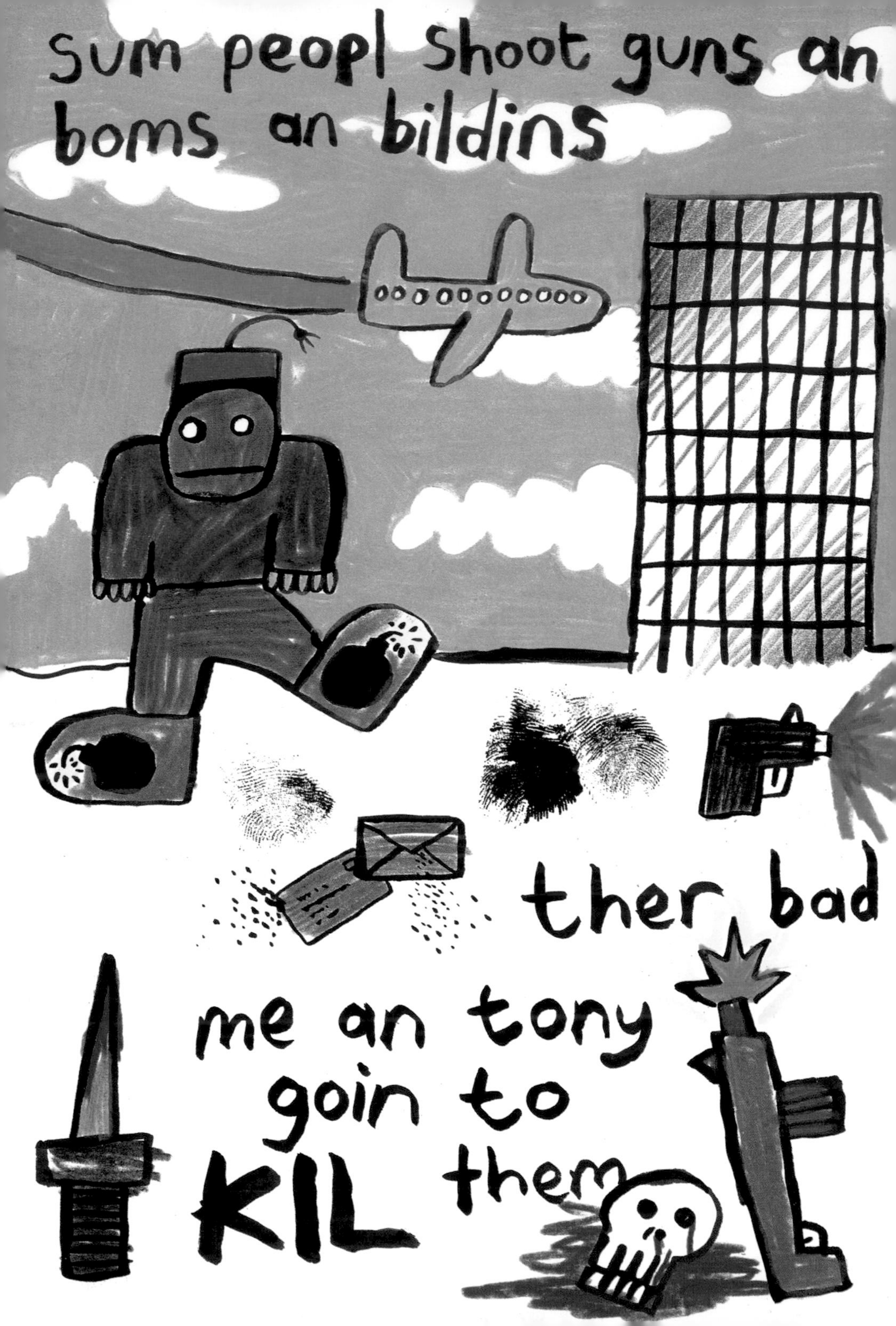
sum peopl shoot guns an boms an bildins
ther bad
me an tony goin to KIL them

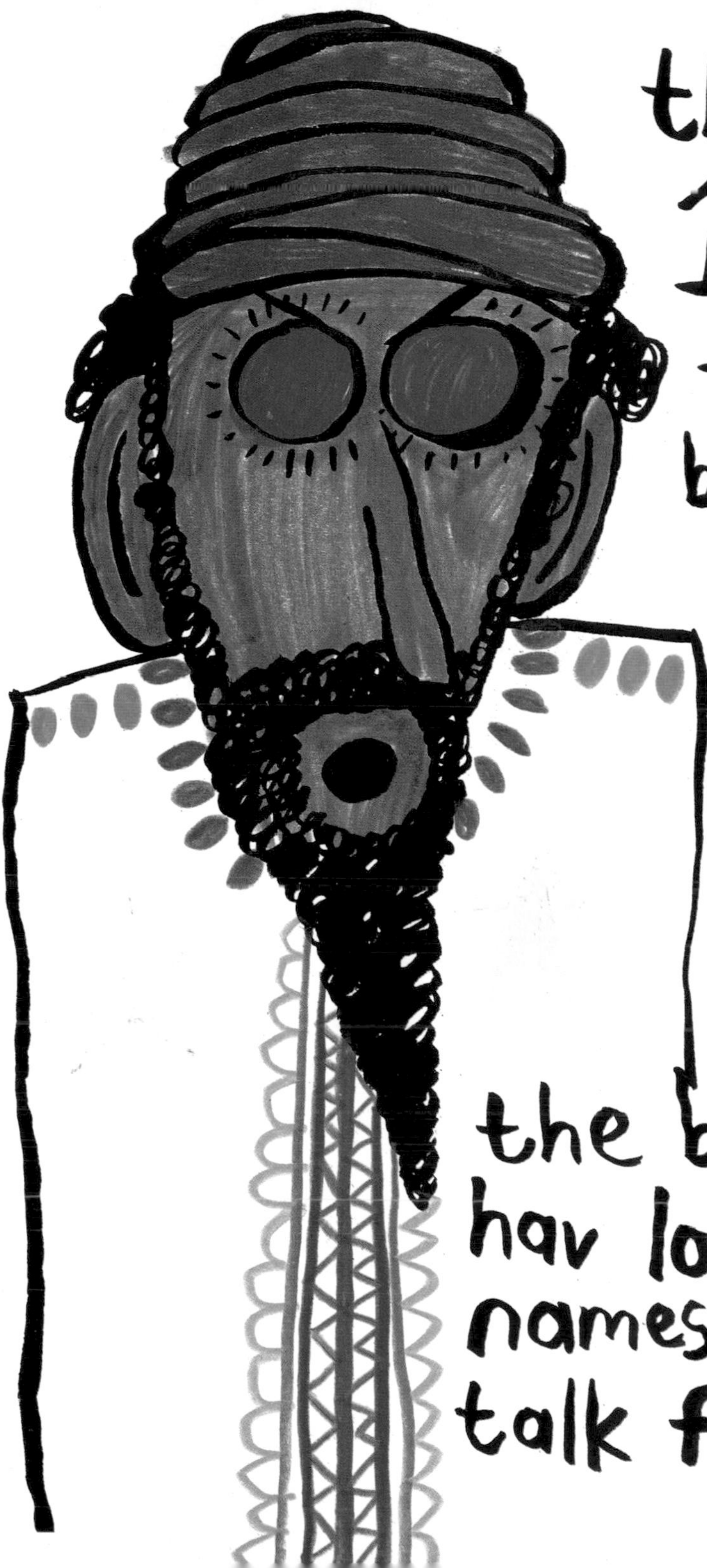

this is 1 of the baddis

the baddis hav long names an talk funy

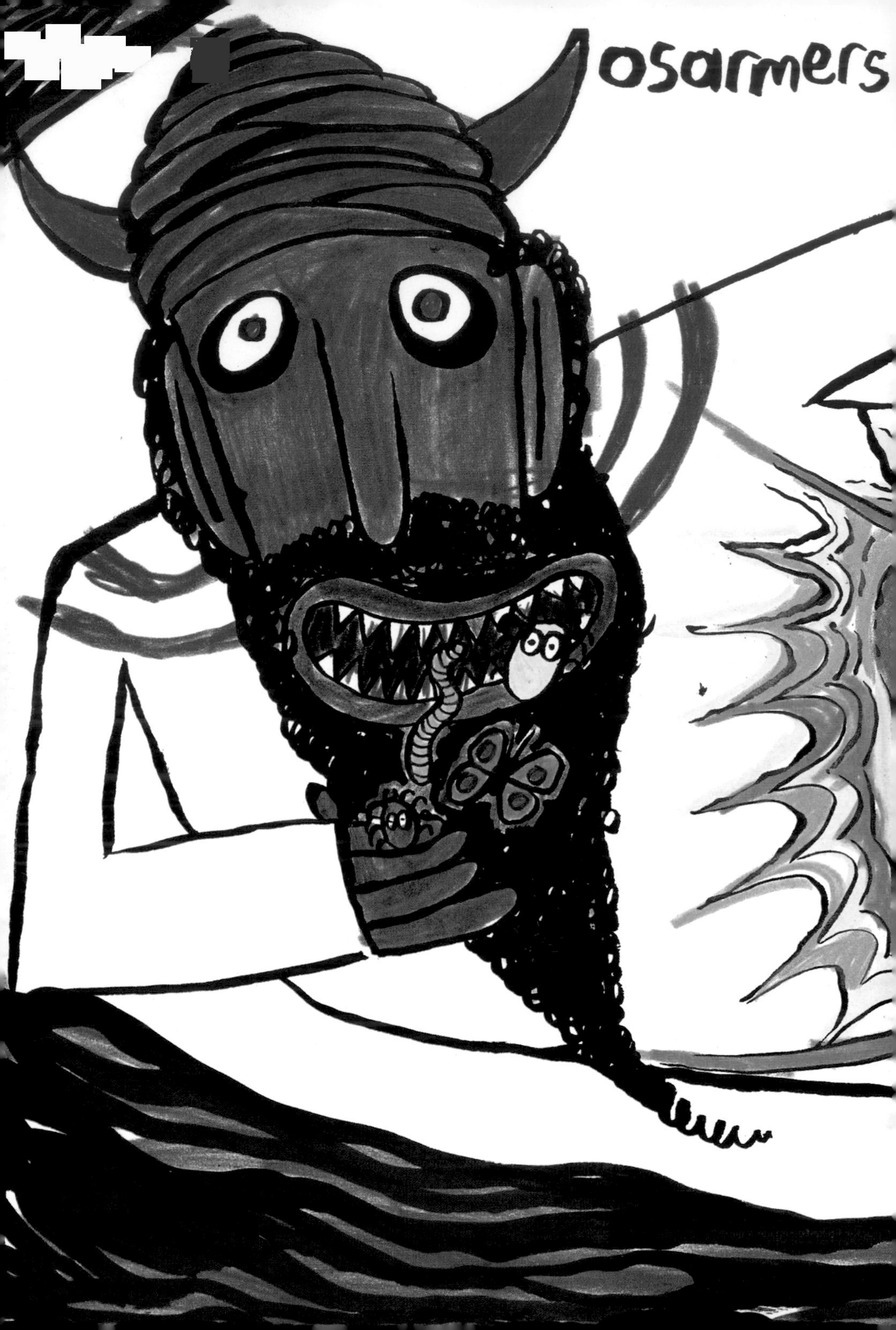
osarmers

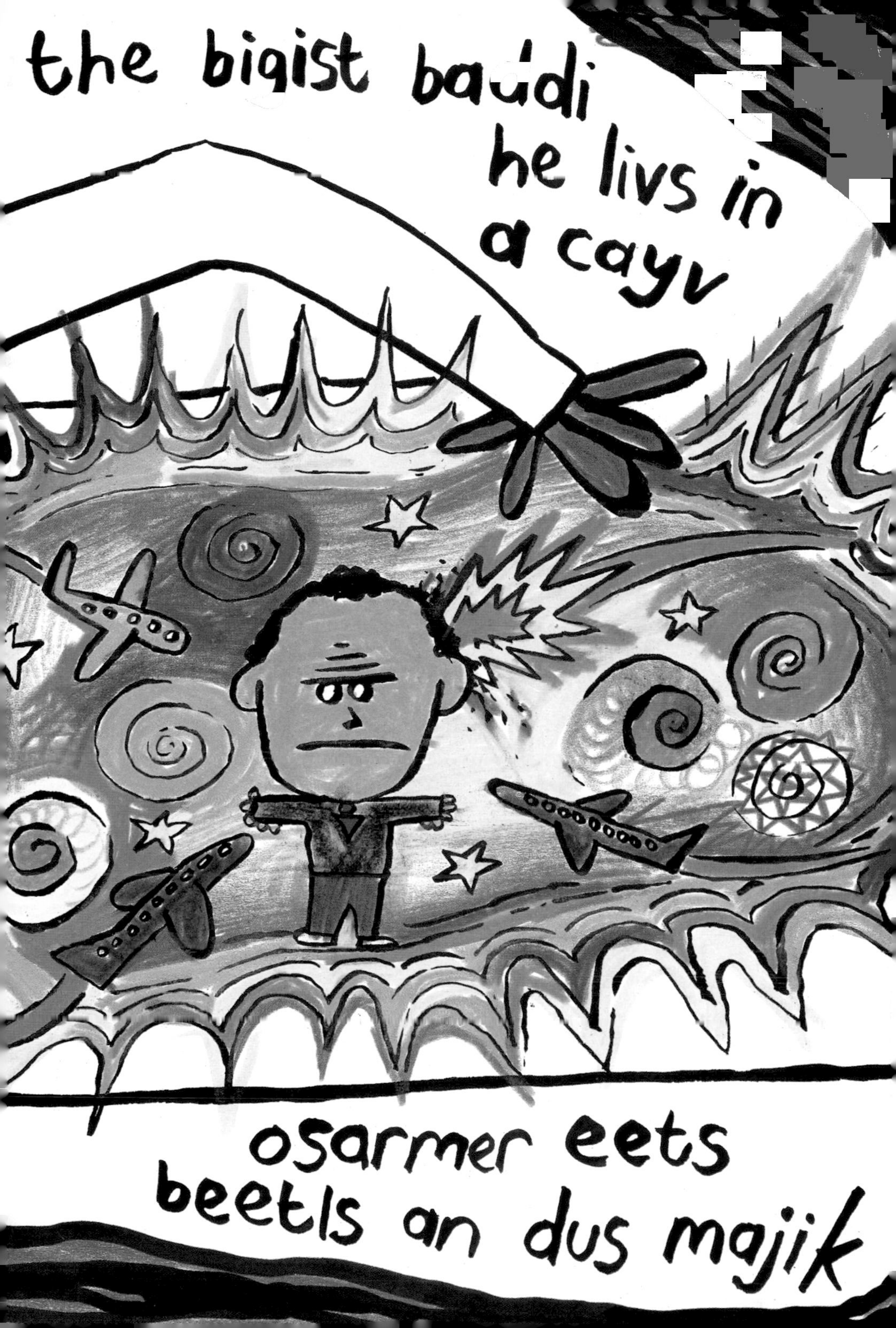
the bigist baddi
he livs in
a cayv
osarmer eets
beetls an dus majik

hes got 4 wiyvs

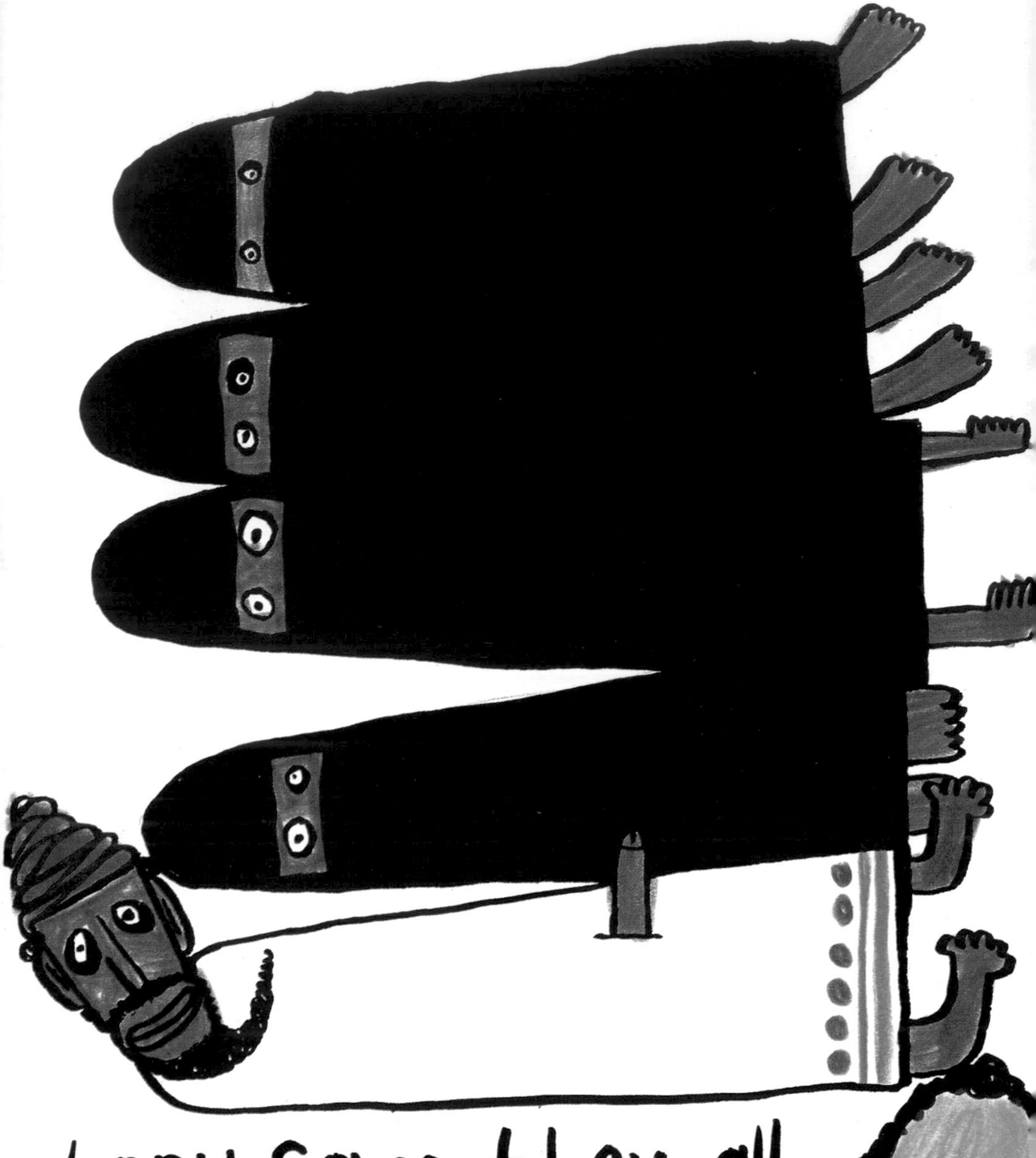

tony says they all do sexin at the same tiem

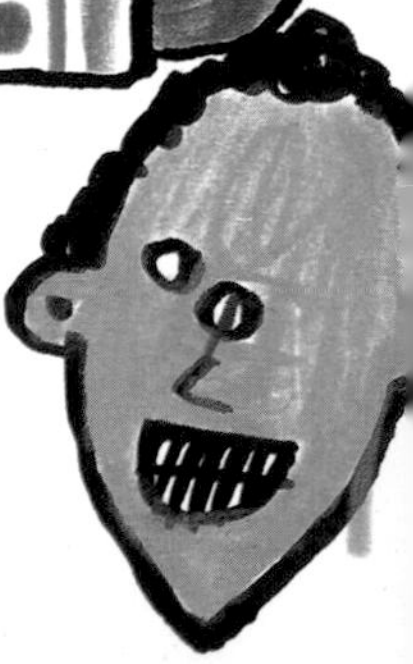

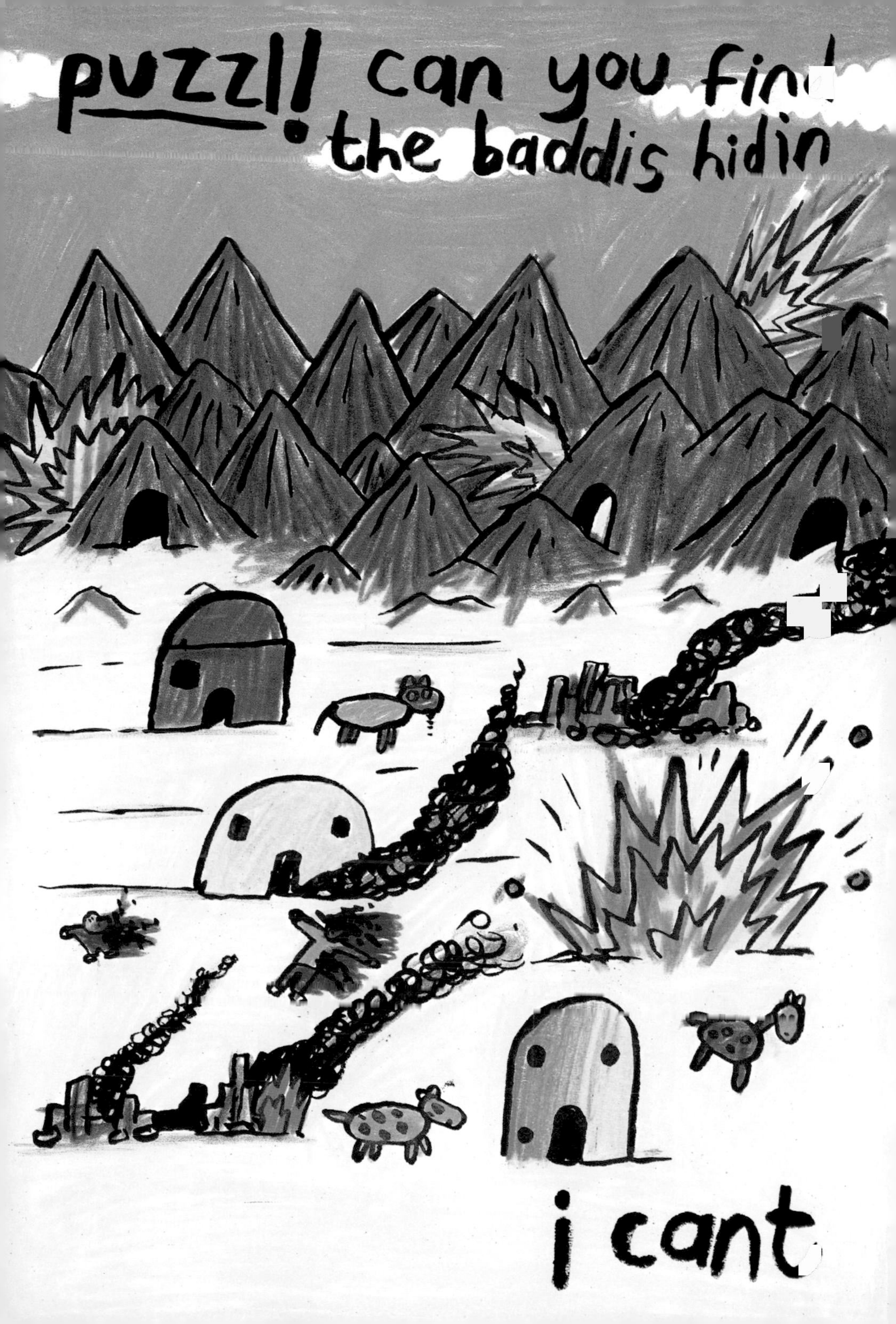
puzzl! can you find the baddis hidin
i cant

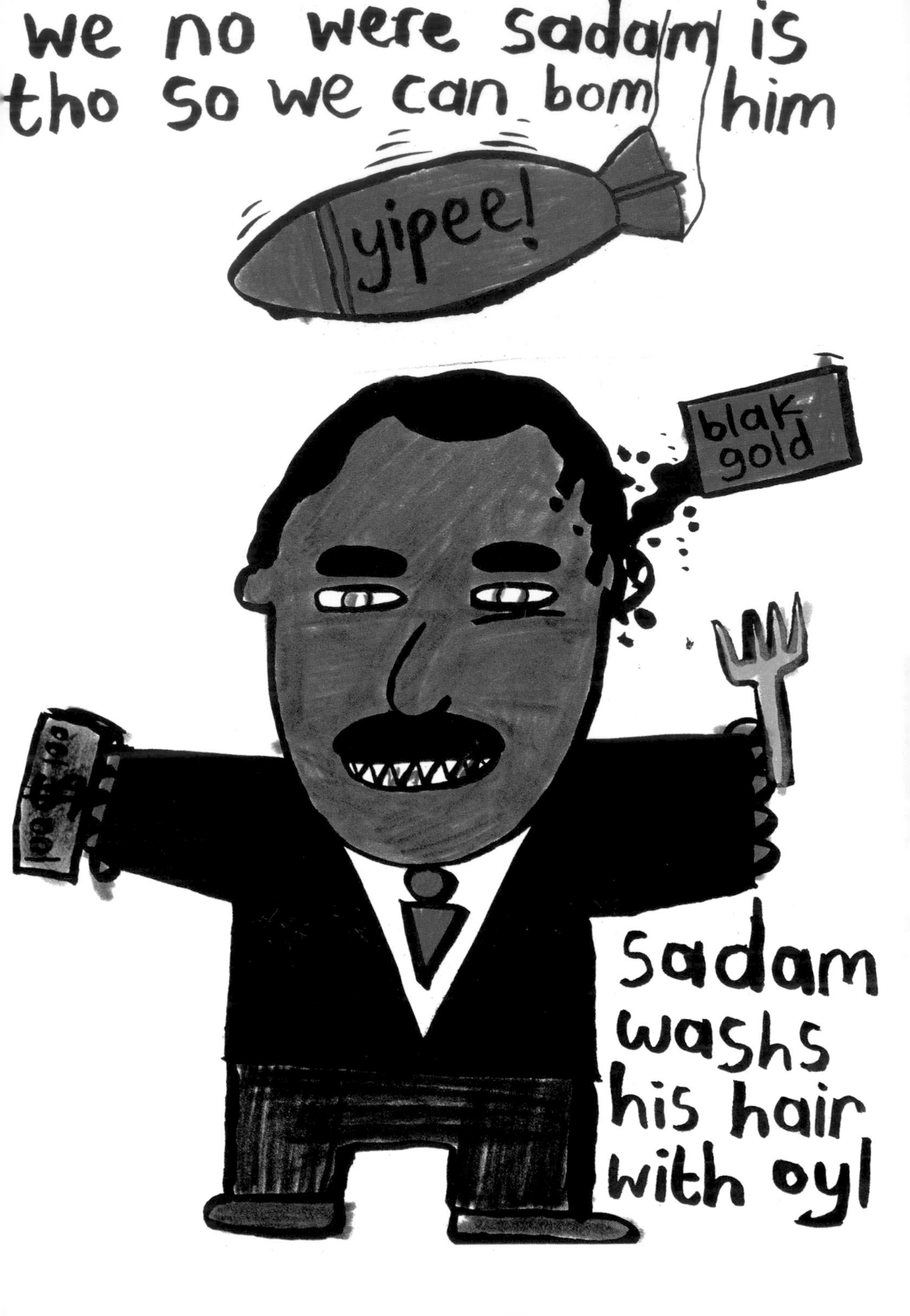
we no were sadam is tho so we can bom him
yipee!
blak gold
sadam washs his hair with oyl

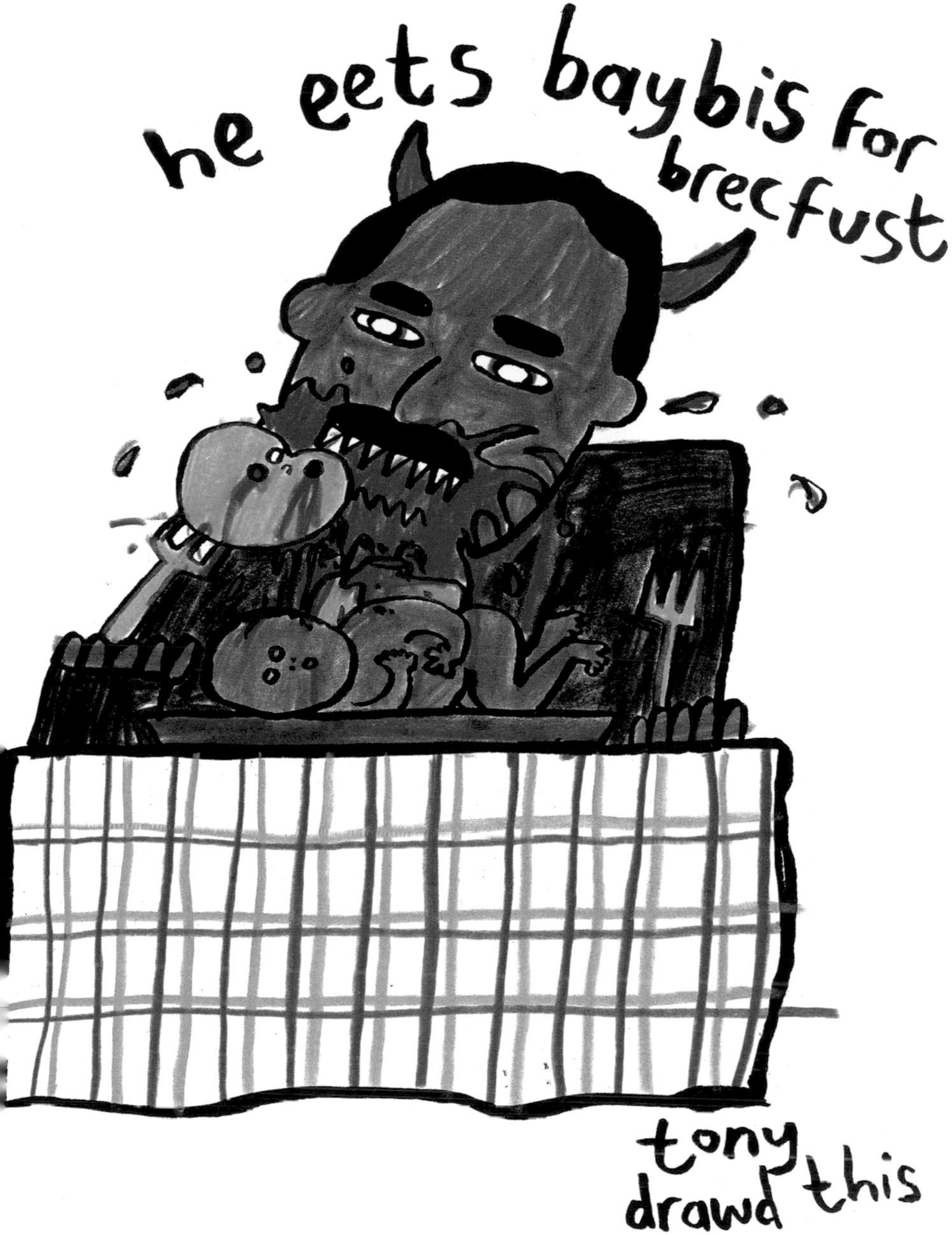
he eets baybis for brecfust
tony drawd this pitur

gun

purson

Sadams tryin to
make the bigist
guns
   he gets his cemiculs
from the boys toylets

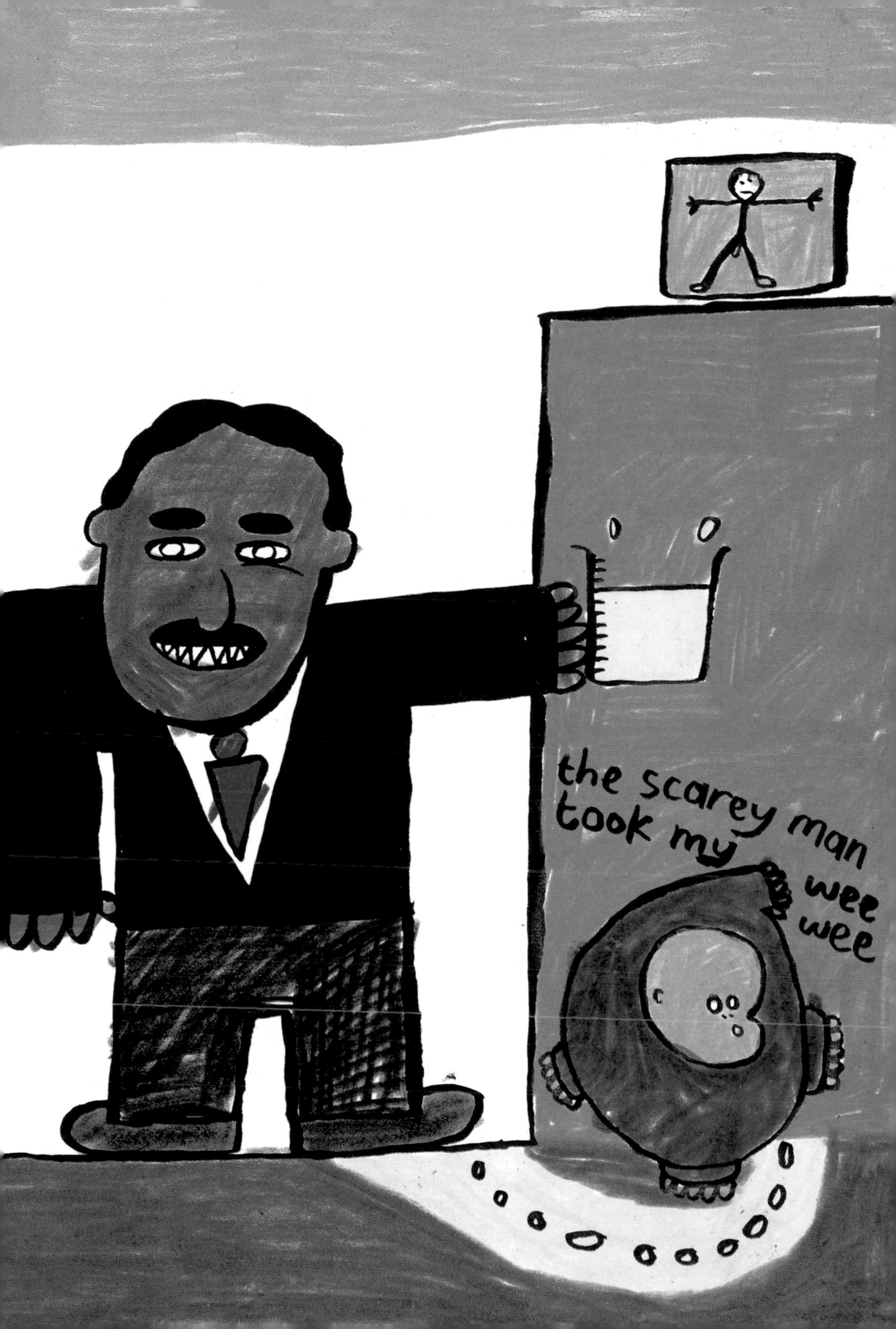
the scarey man took my wee wee

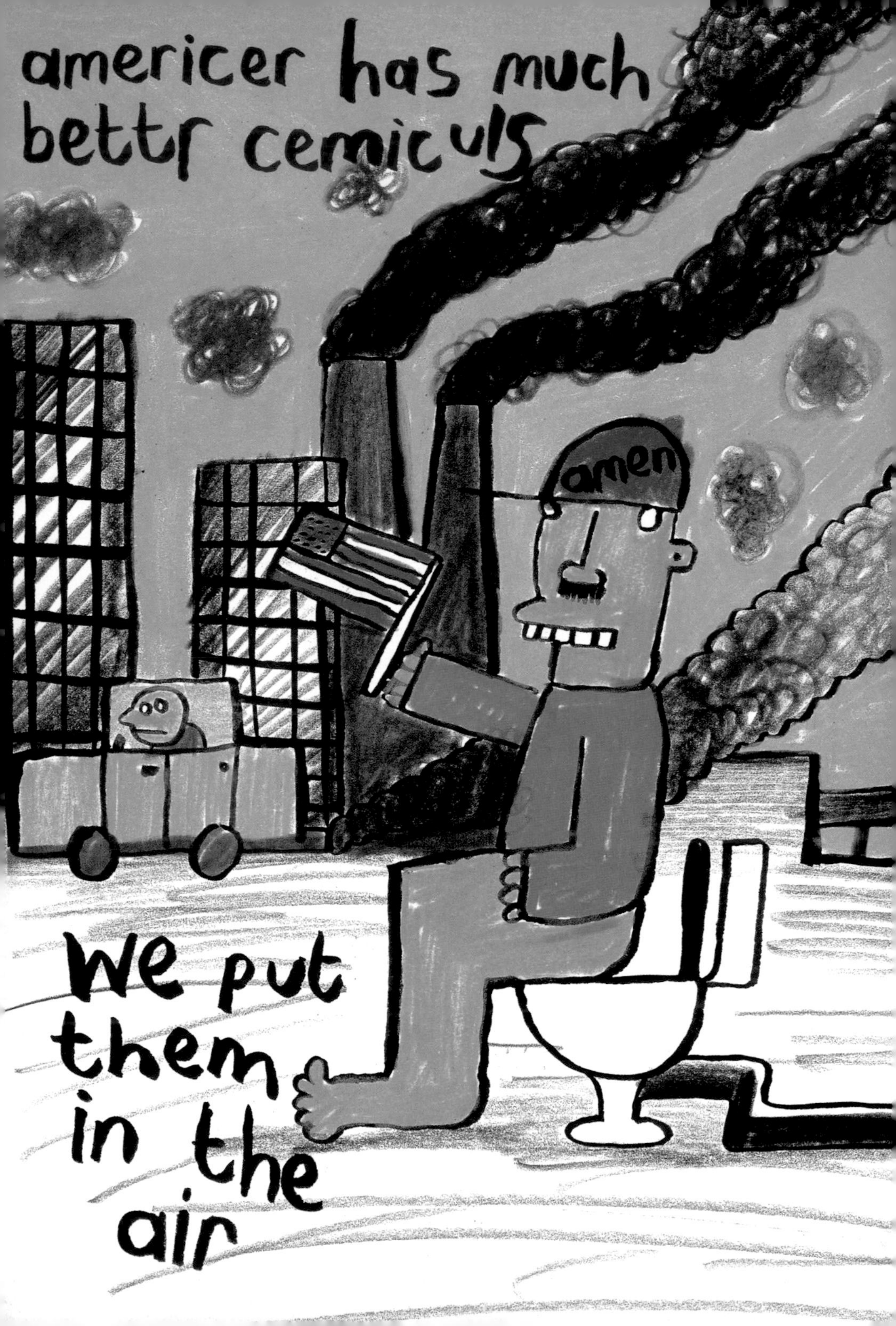
americer has much
bettr cemiculs
amen
We put
them
in the
air

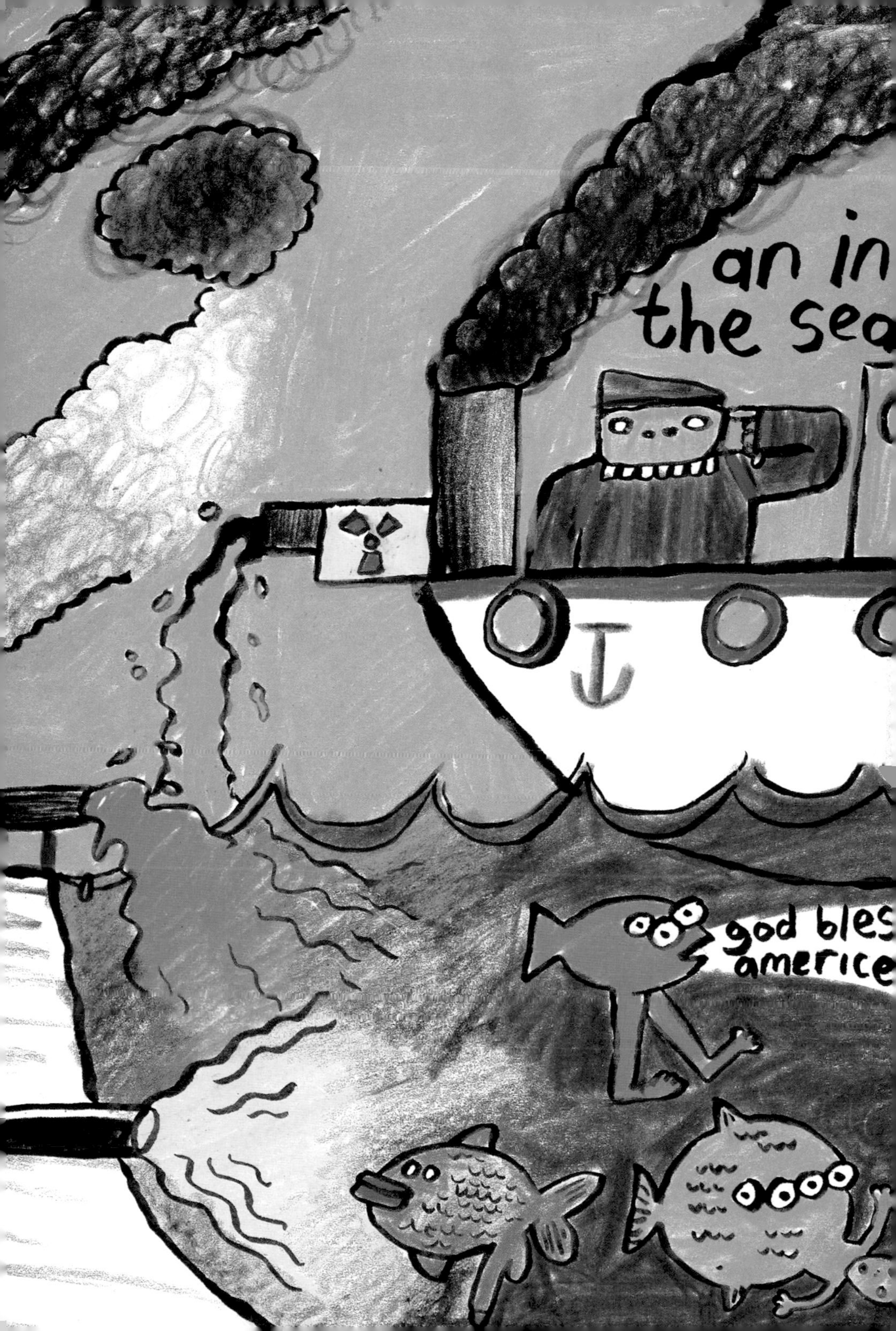
an in
the sea
god bles
americe

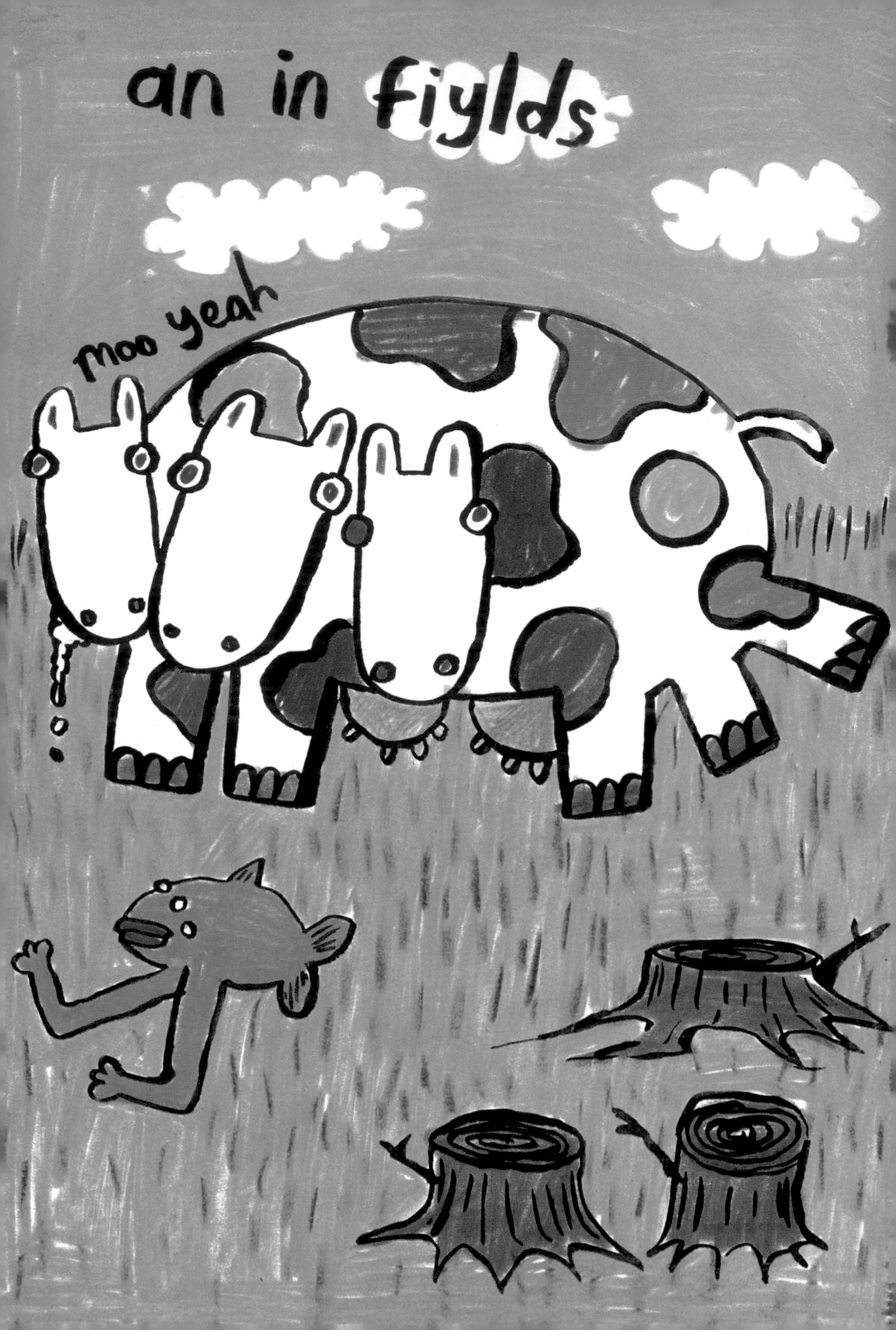
an in fiylds
moo yeah

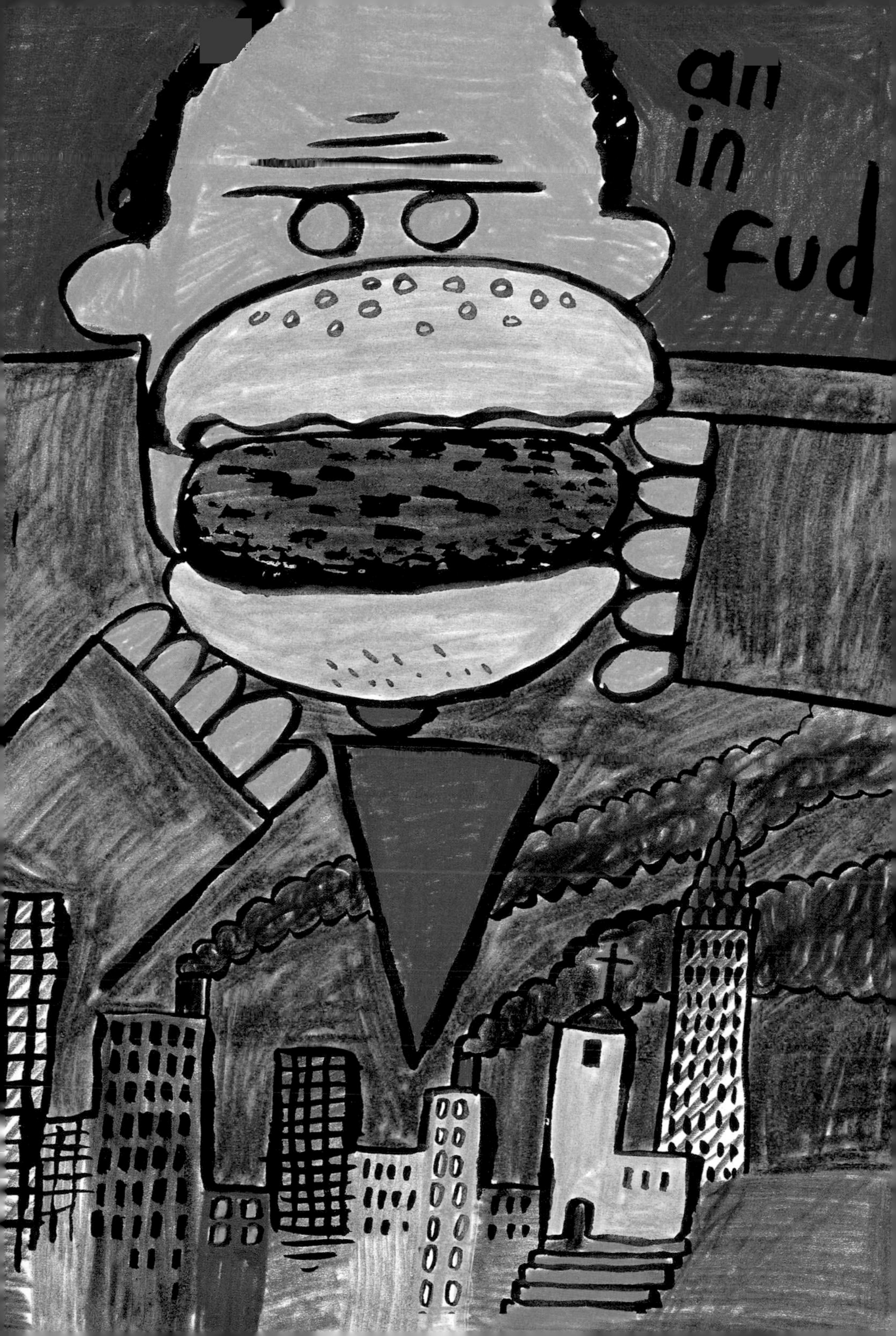
an
in
Fud

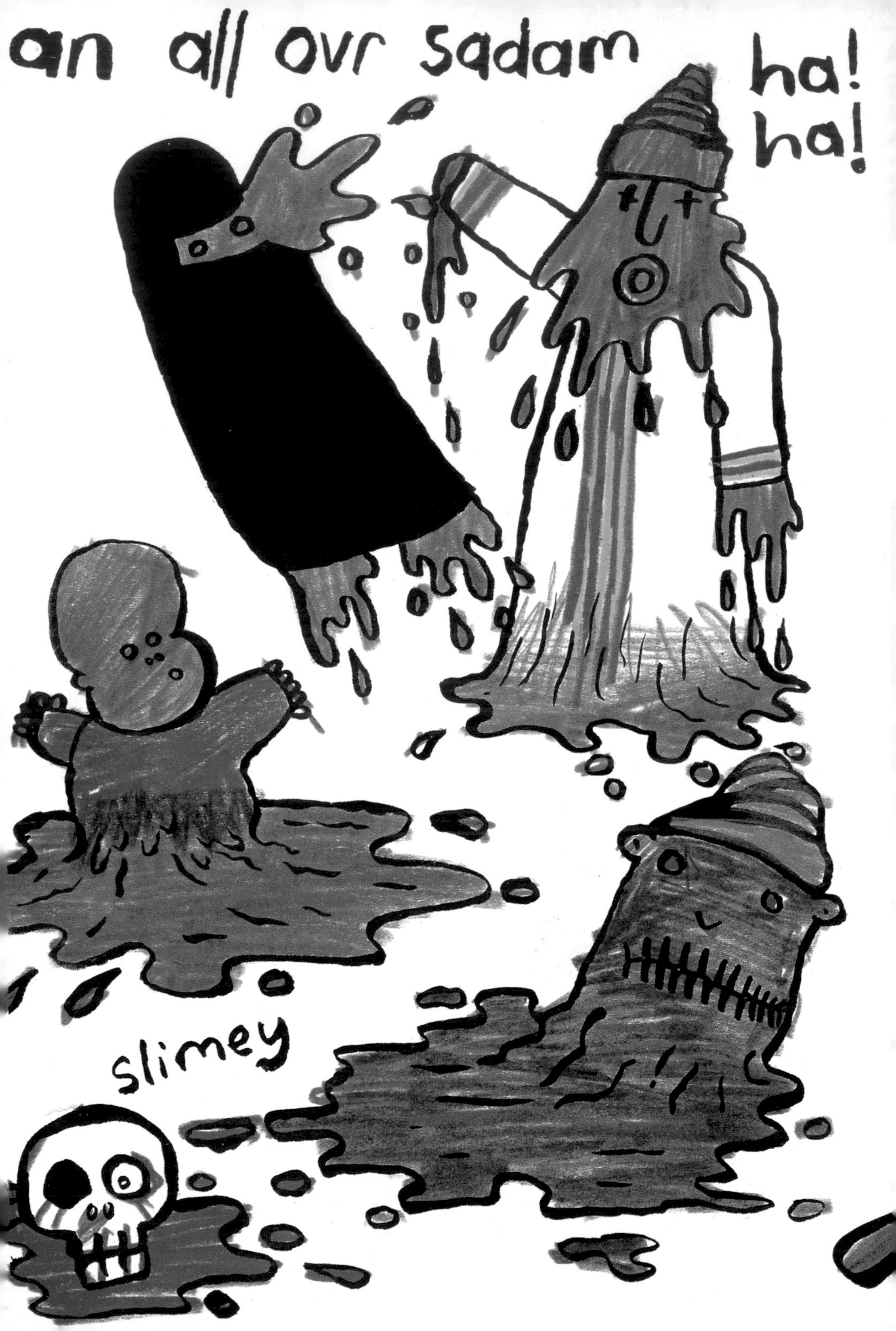
an all ovr sadam
ha! ha!
slimey

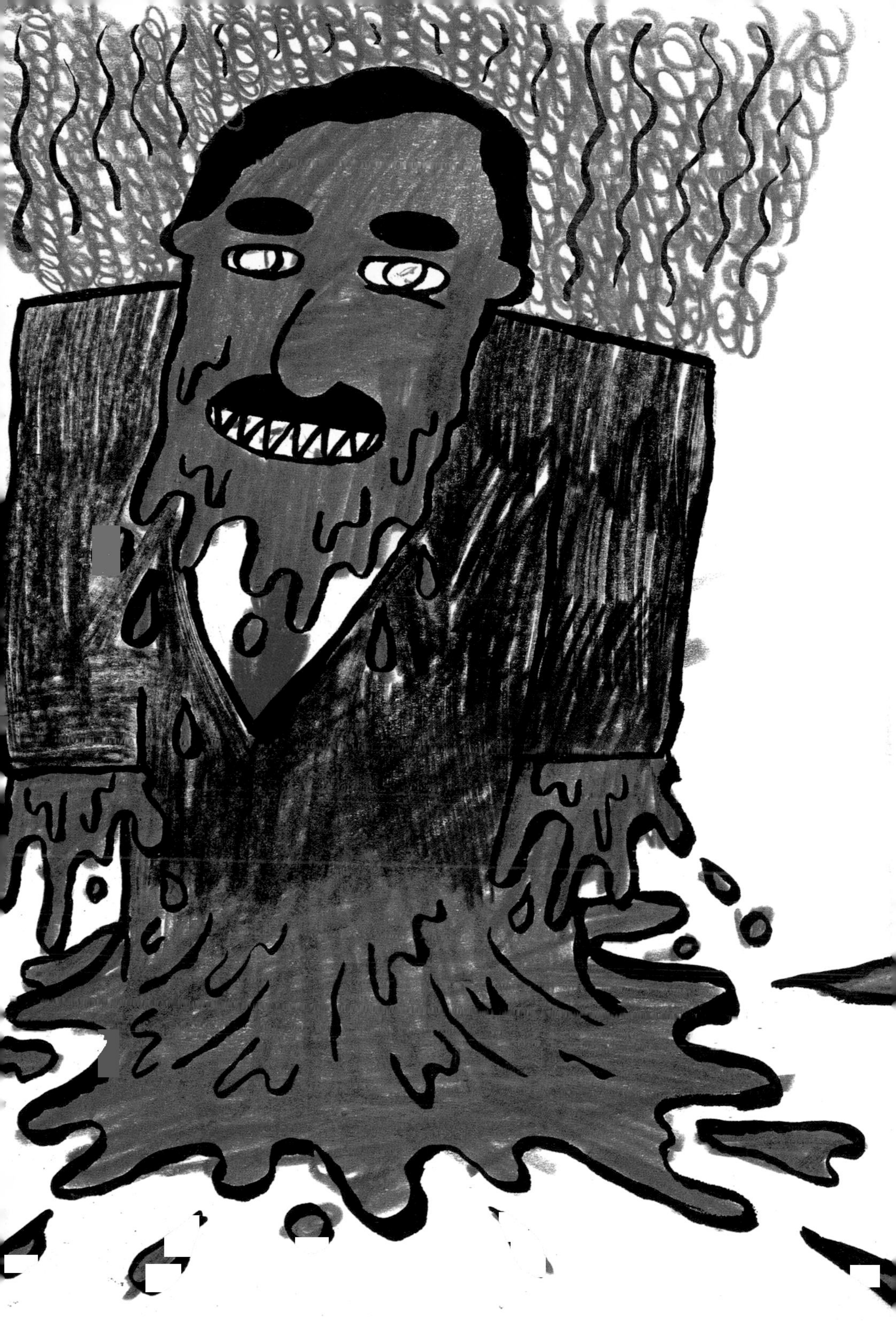

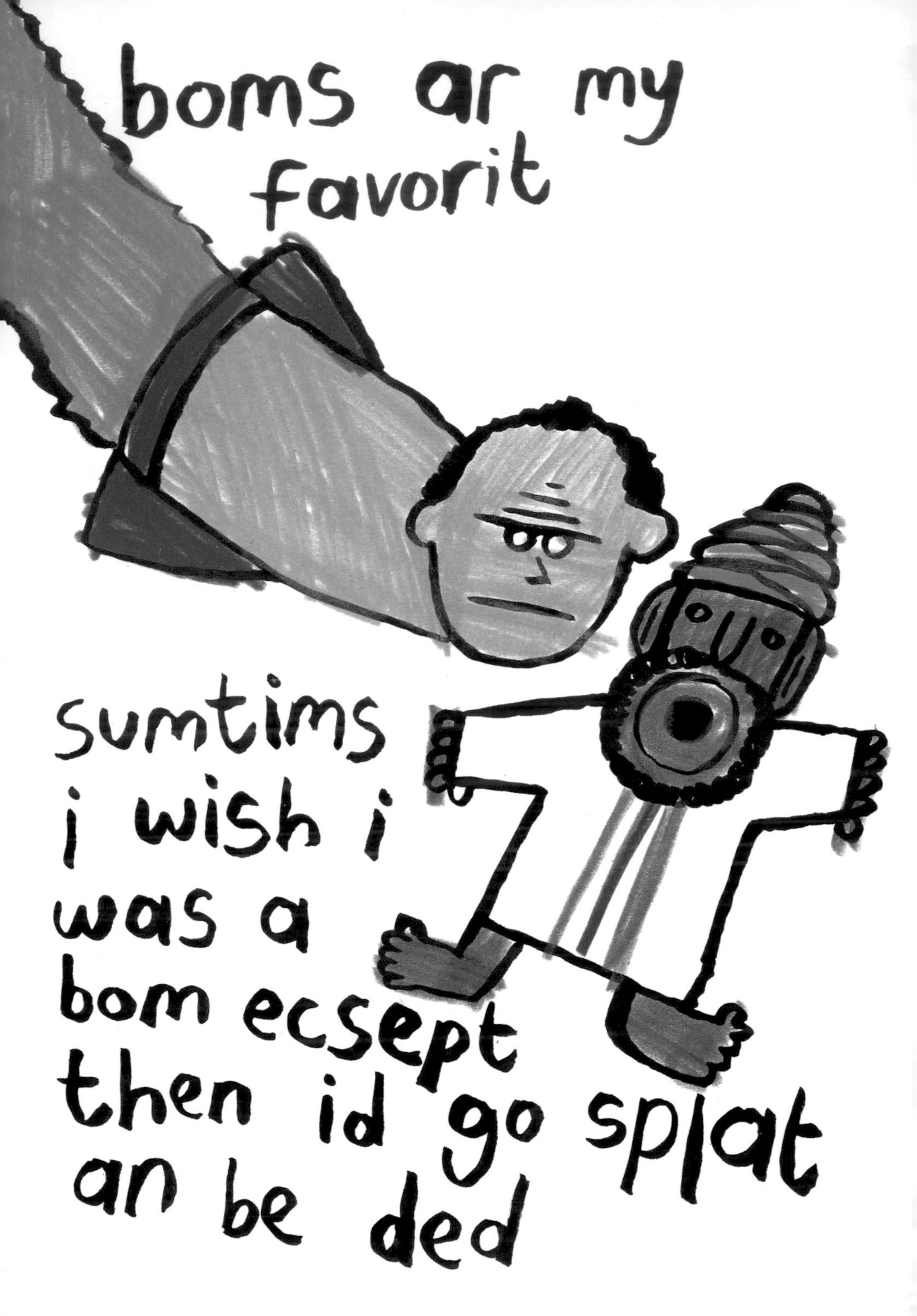
boms ar my favorit
sumtims i wish i was a bom ecsept then id go splat an be ded

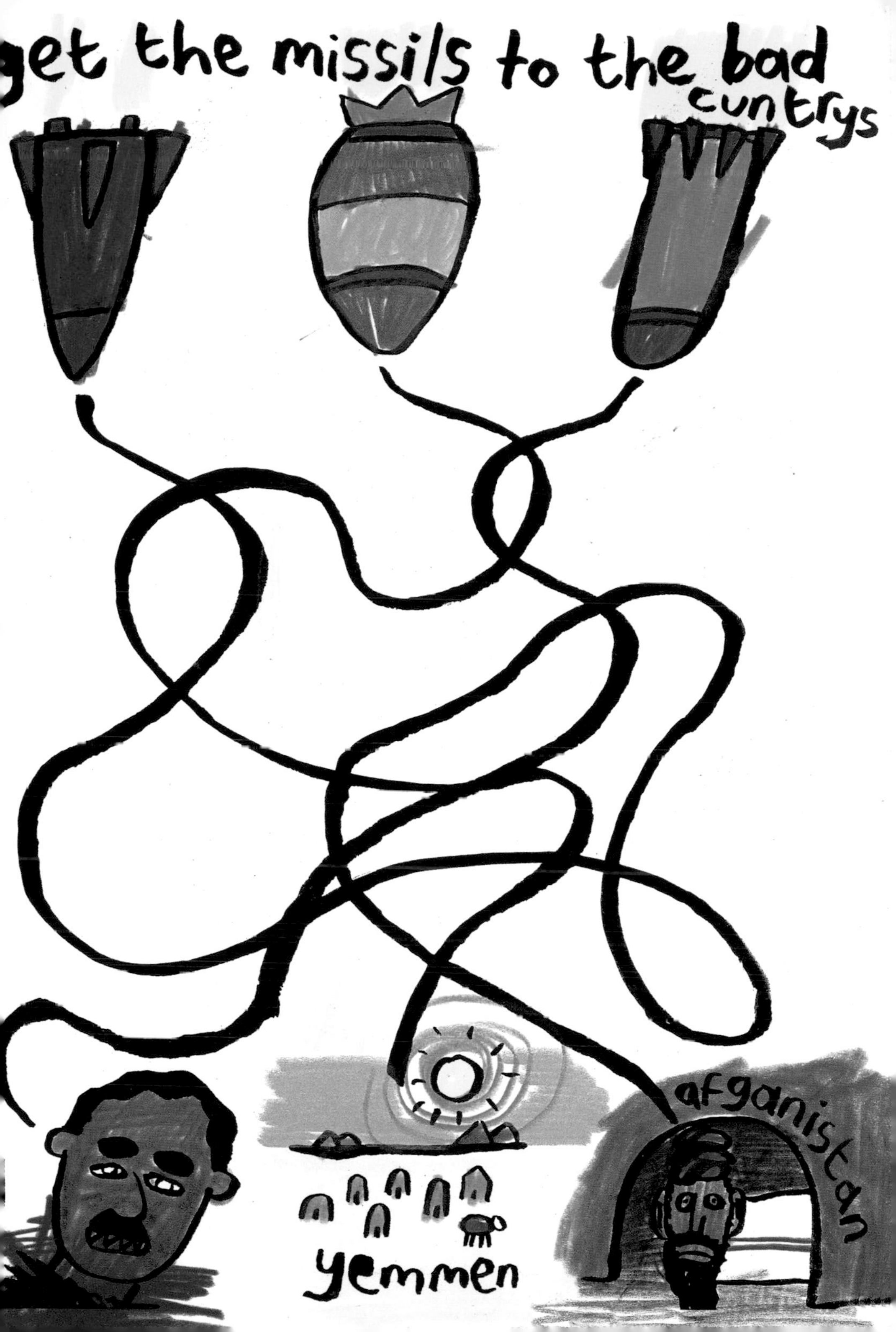
get the missils to the bad cuntrys
afganistan
yemmen

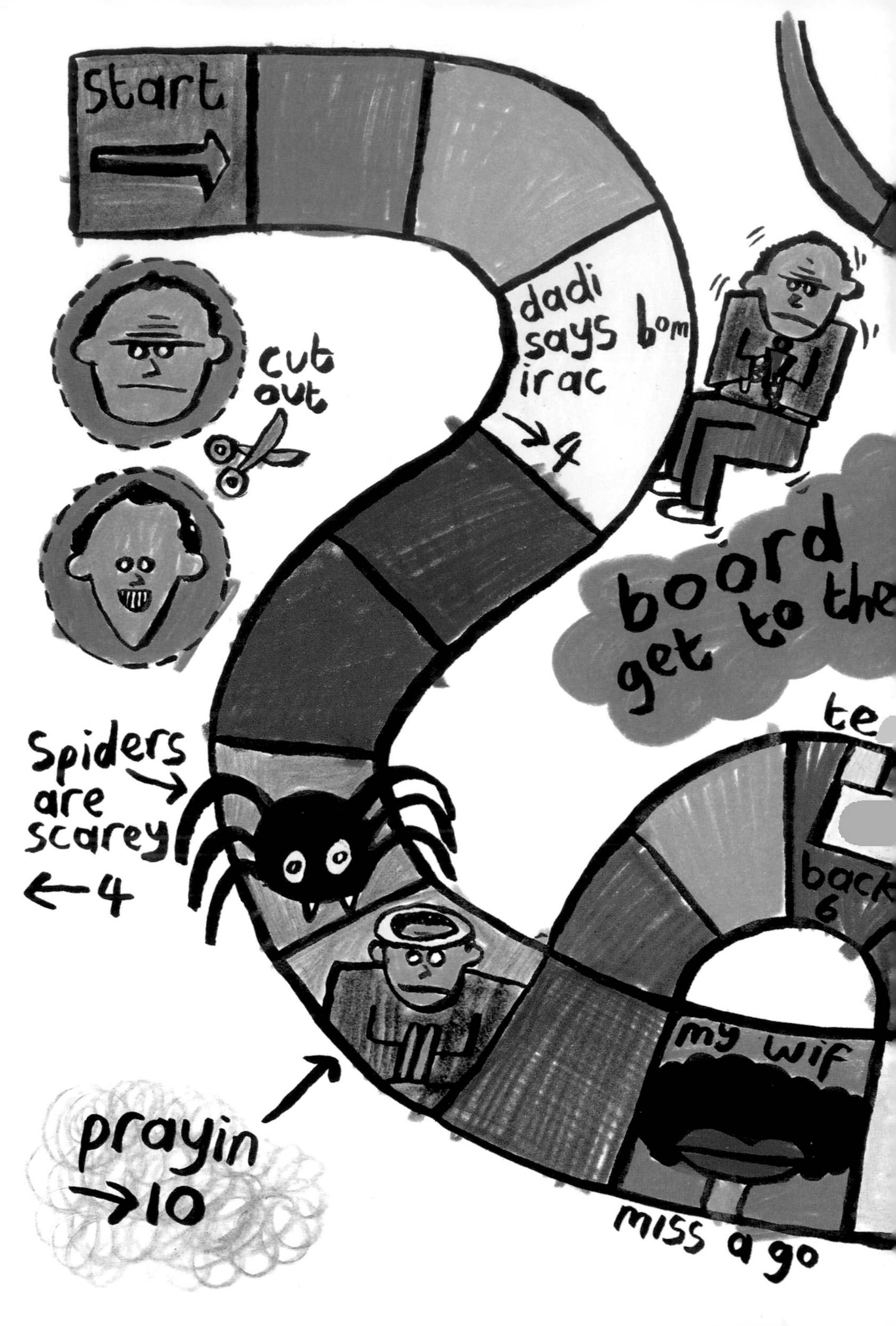
Start
dadi says bom irac →4
cut out
boord
get to the
Spiders are scarey ←4
back 6
my wif
miss a go
prayin →10

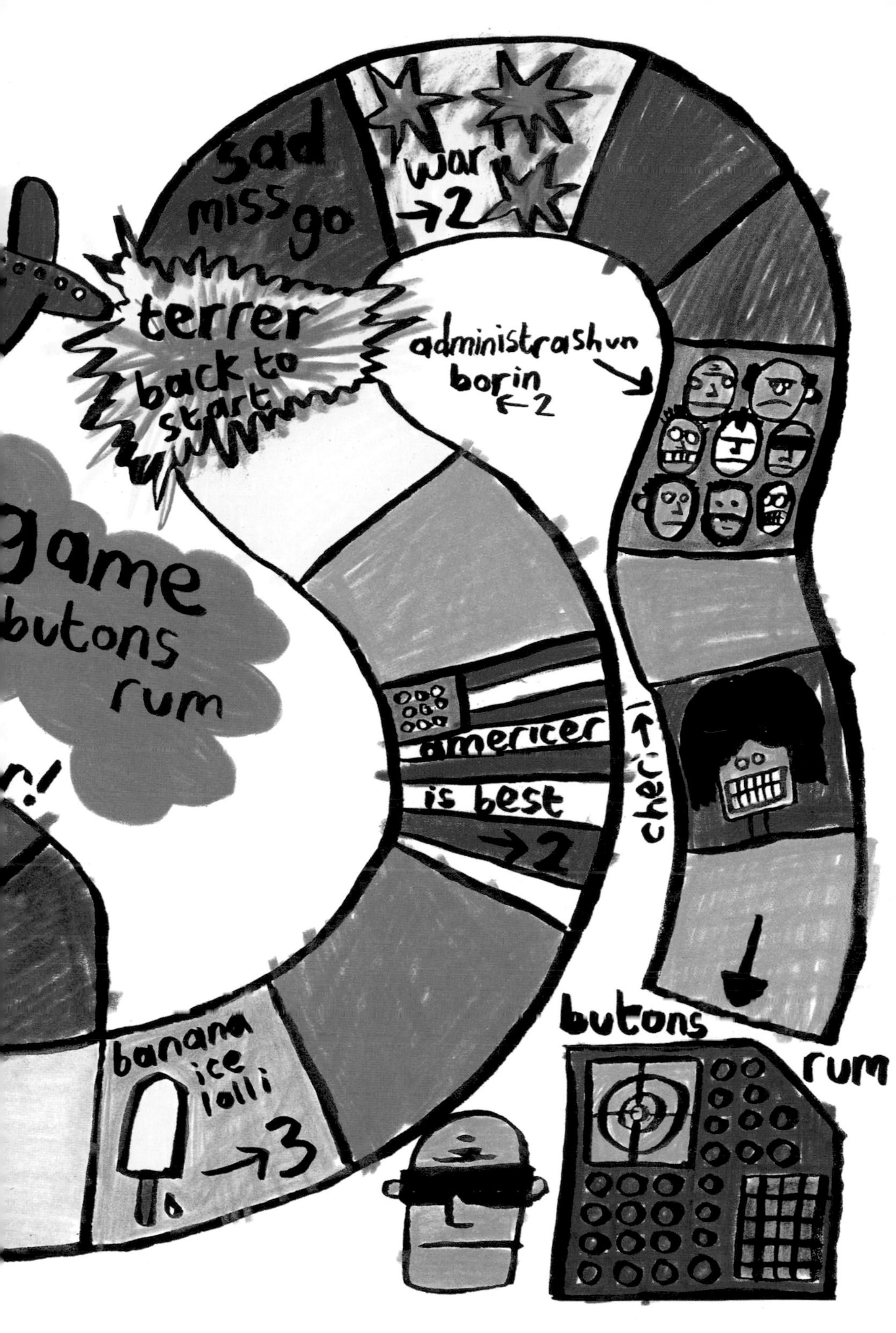
sad miss go
war →2
terrer back to start
administrashun borin ←2
game butons rum
r!
americer is best →2
cheri
banana ice lolli →3
butons rum

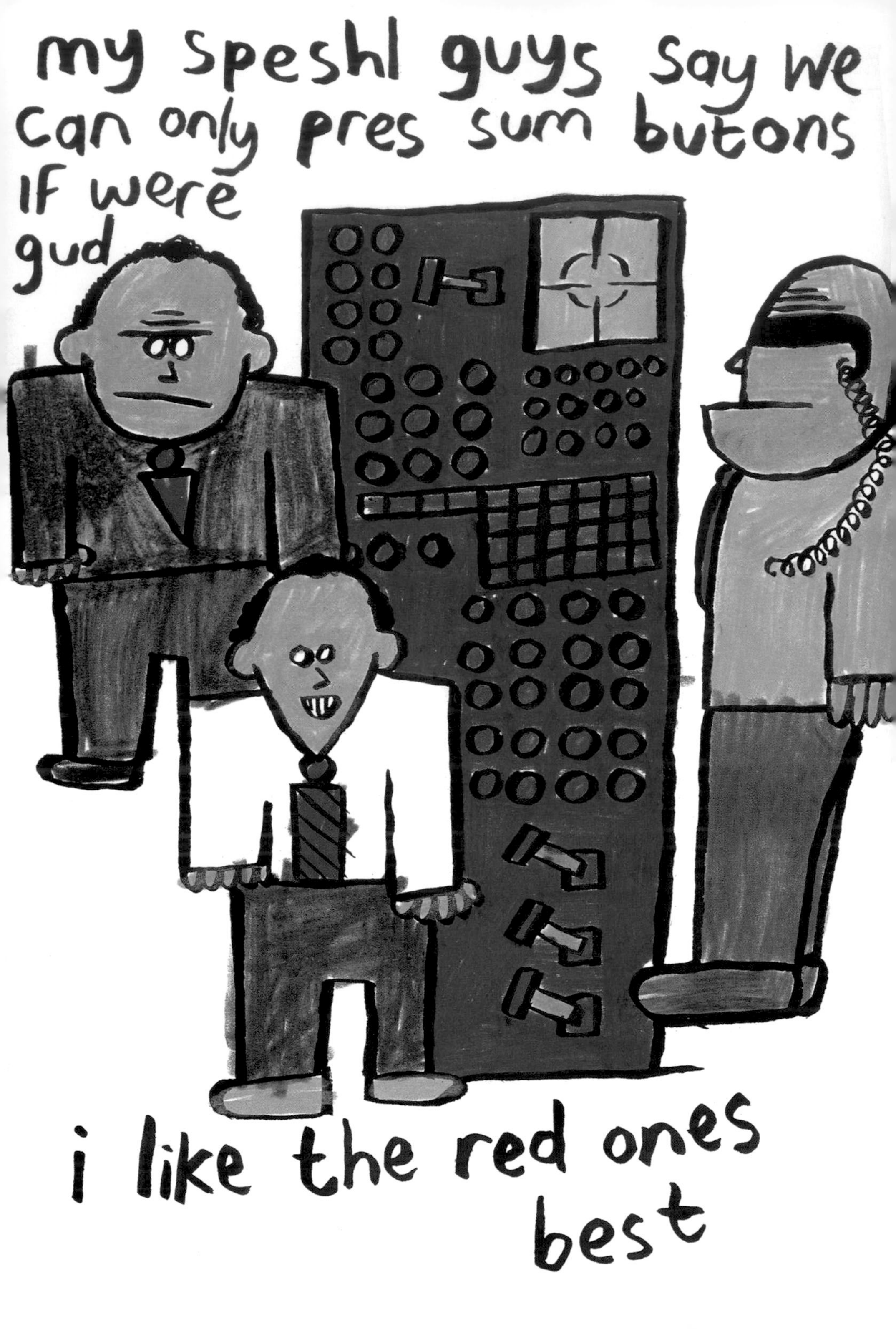
my speshl guys say we can only pres sum butons if were gud
i like the red ones best

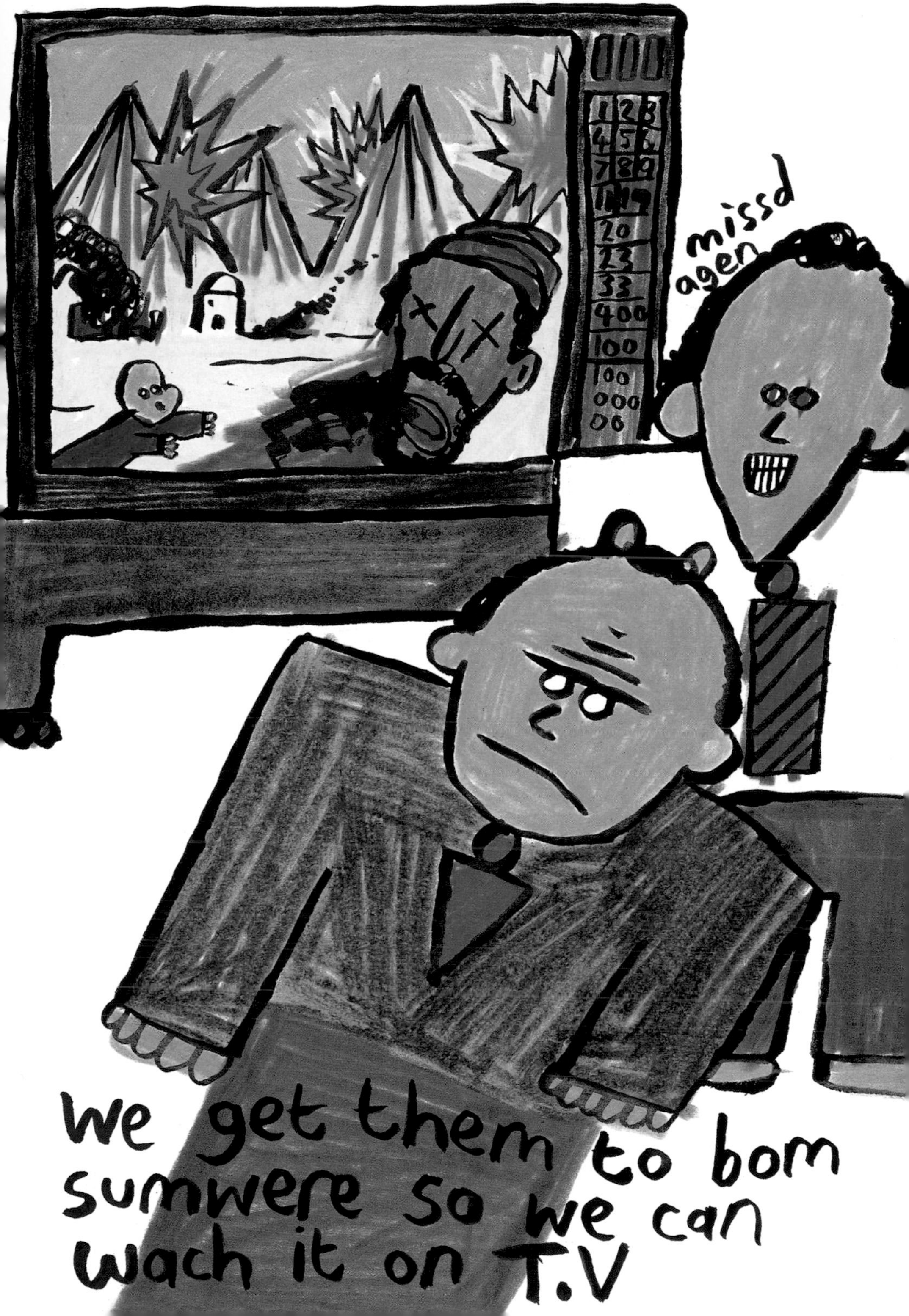
missd agen
We get them to bom sumwere so we can wach it on T.V

we make camps like on T.V
im the acsis of evil

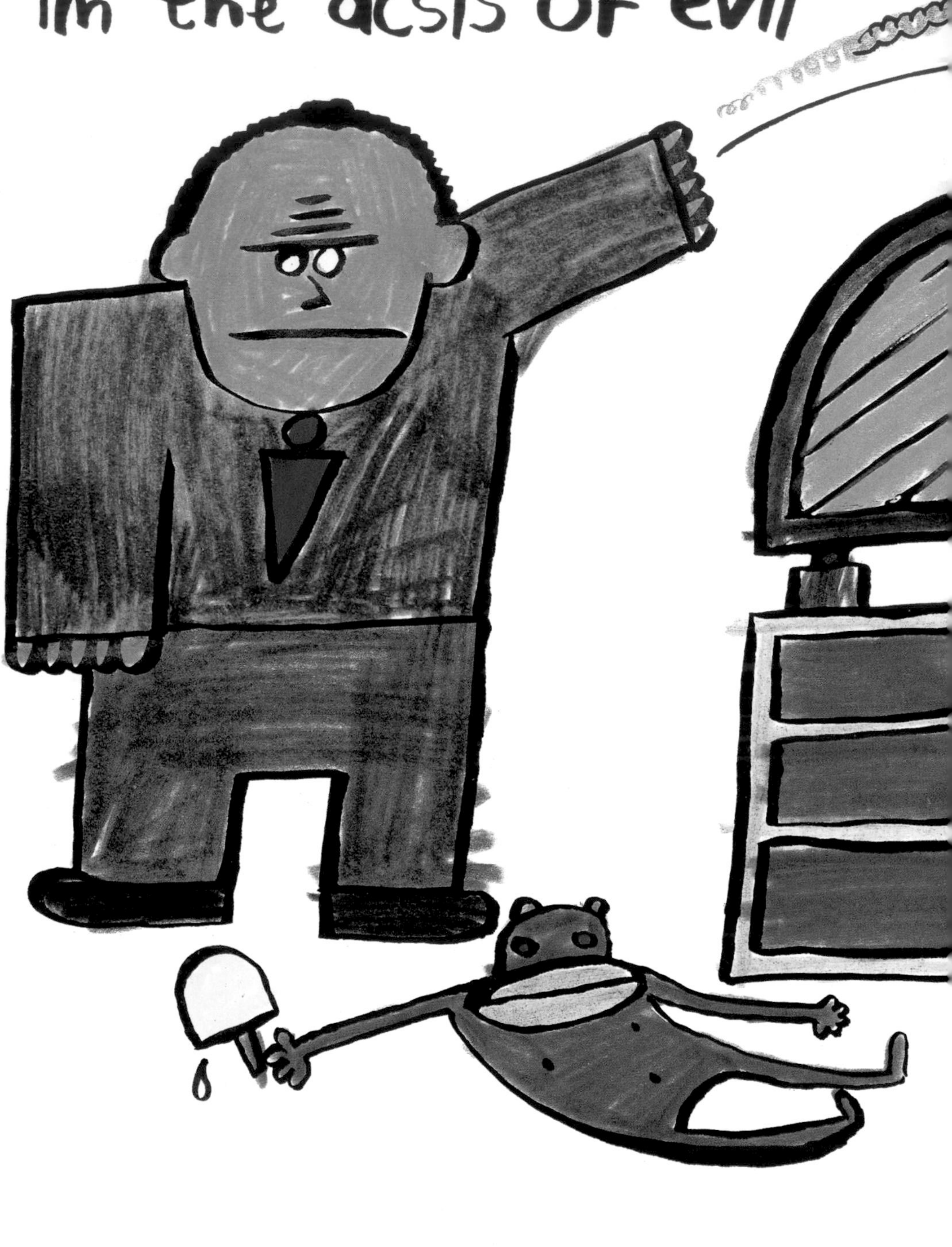

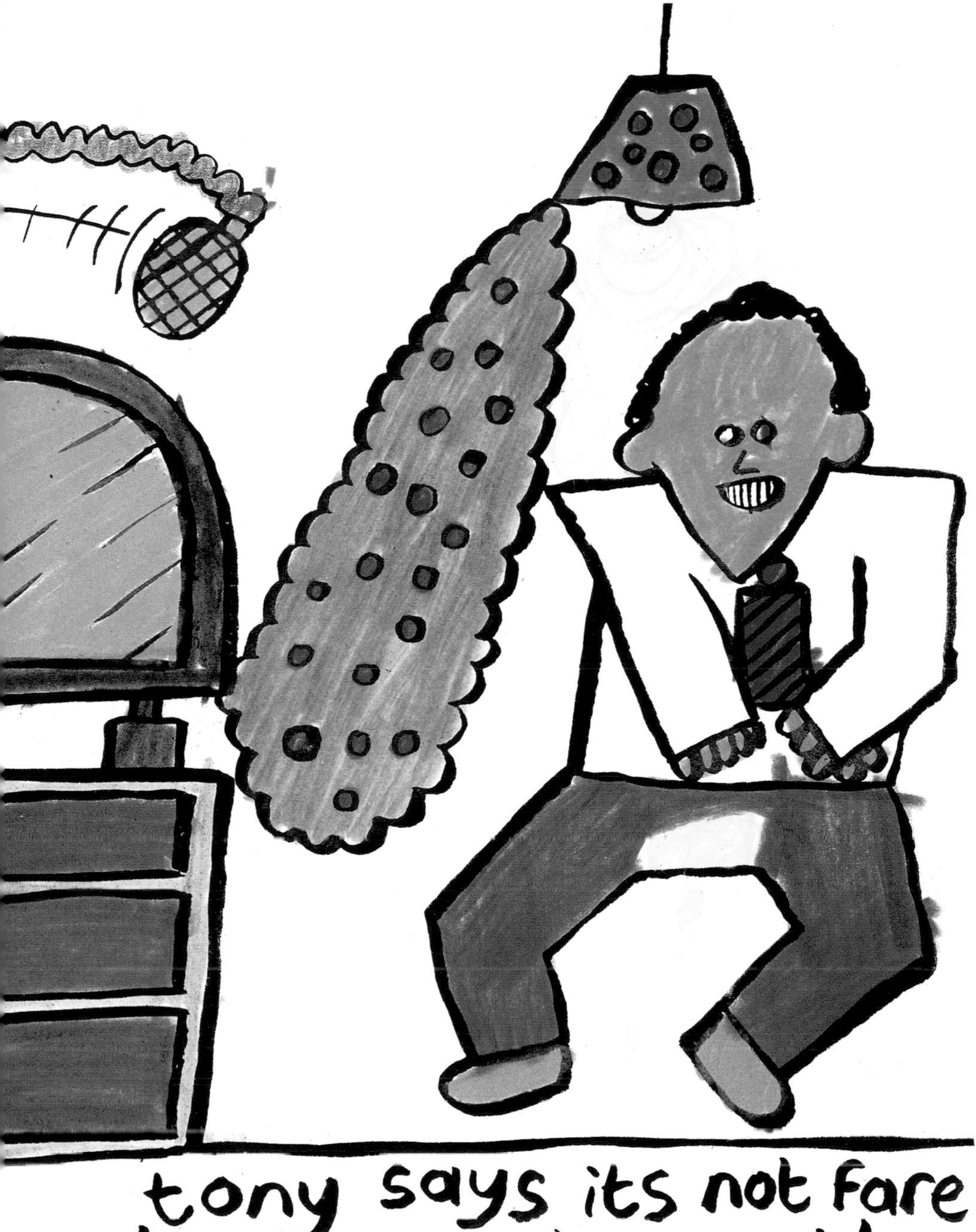

tony says its not fare
becaus iv got grenaids
an mr munky. mr munky
likes banana ice lolis

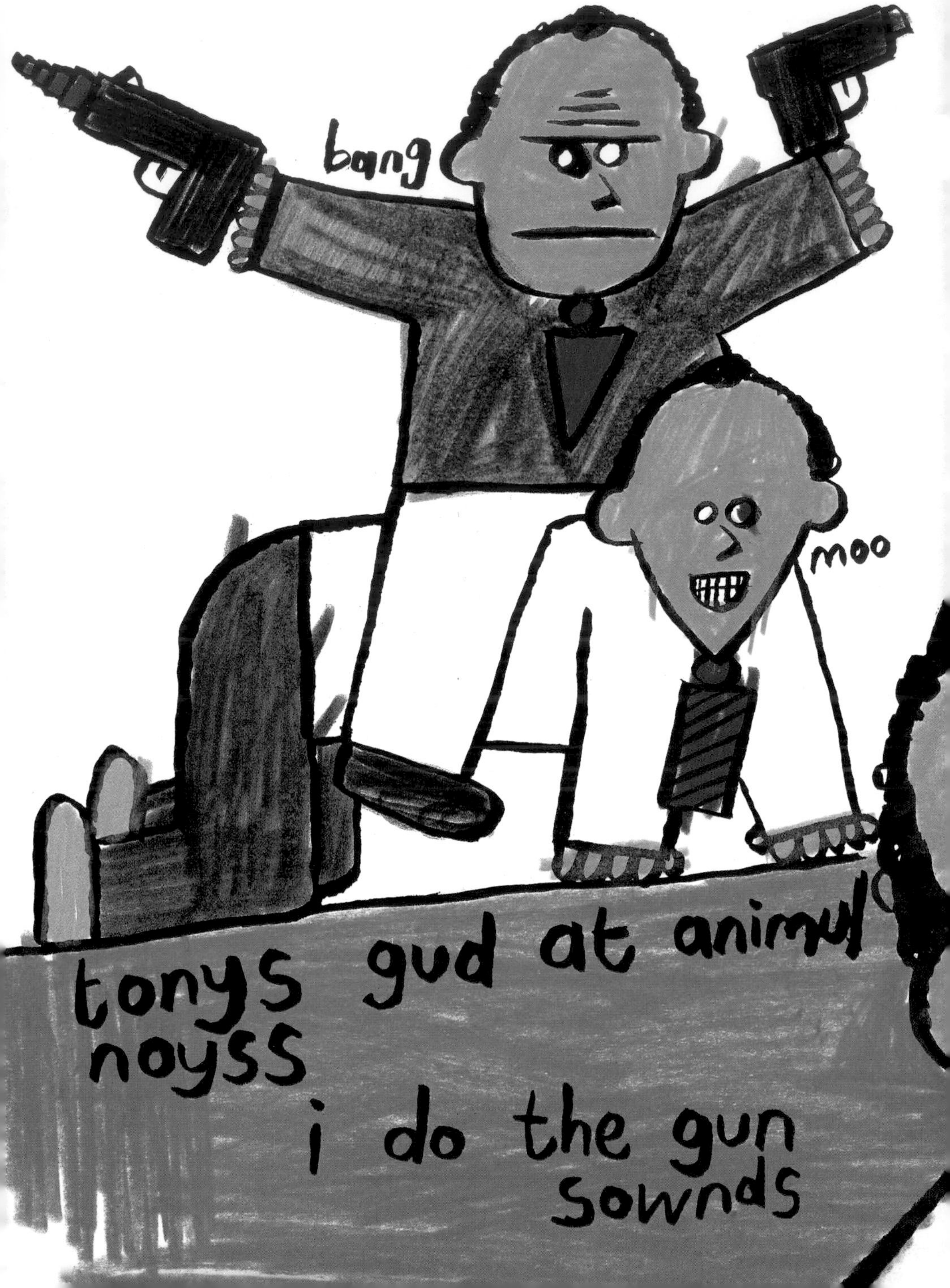
bang
moo
tonys gud at animul noyss
i do the gun sownds

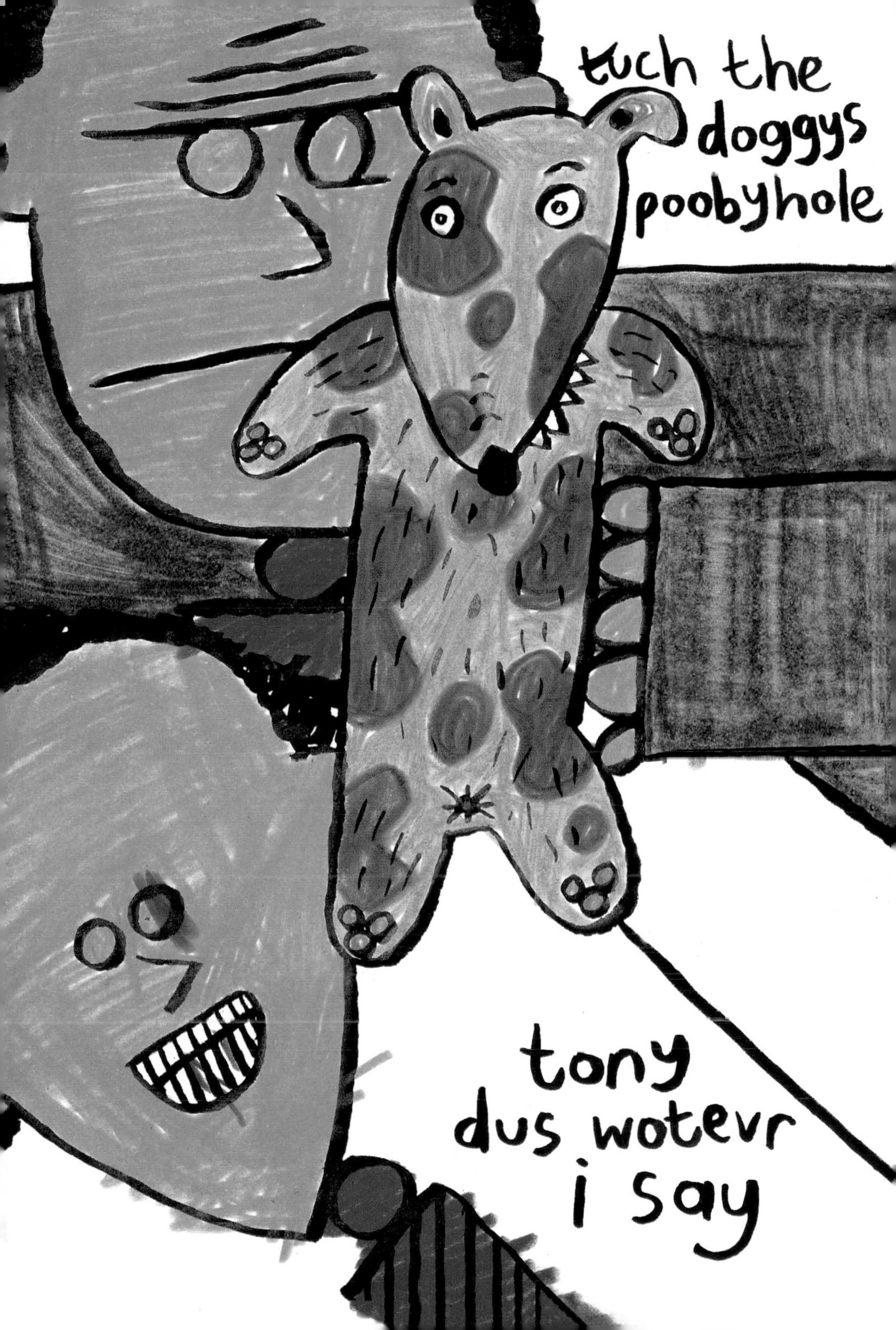
tuch the doggys poobyhole
tony dus wotevr i say

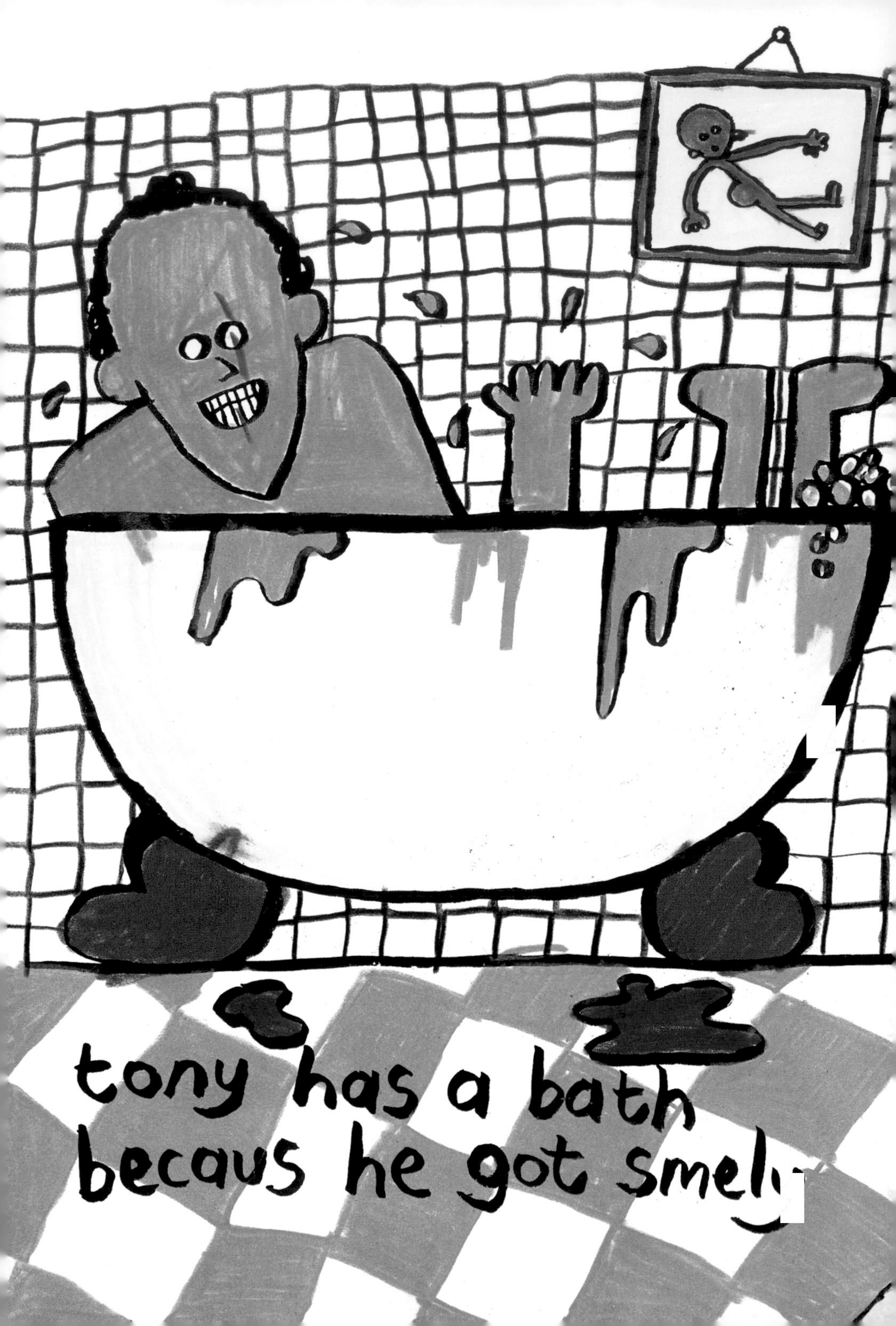
tony has a bath
becaus he got smely

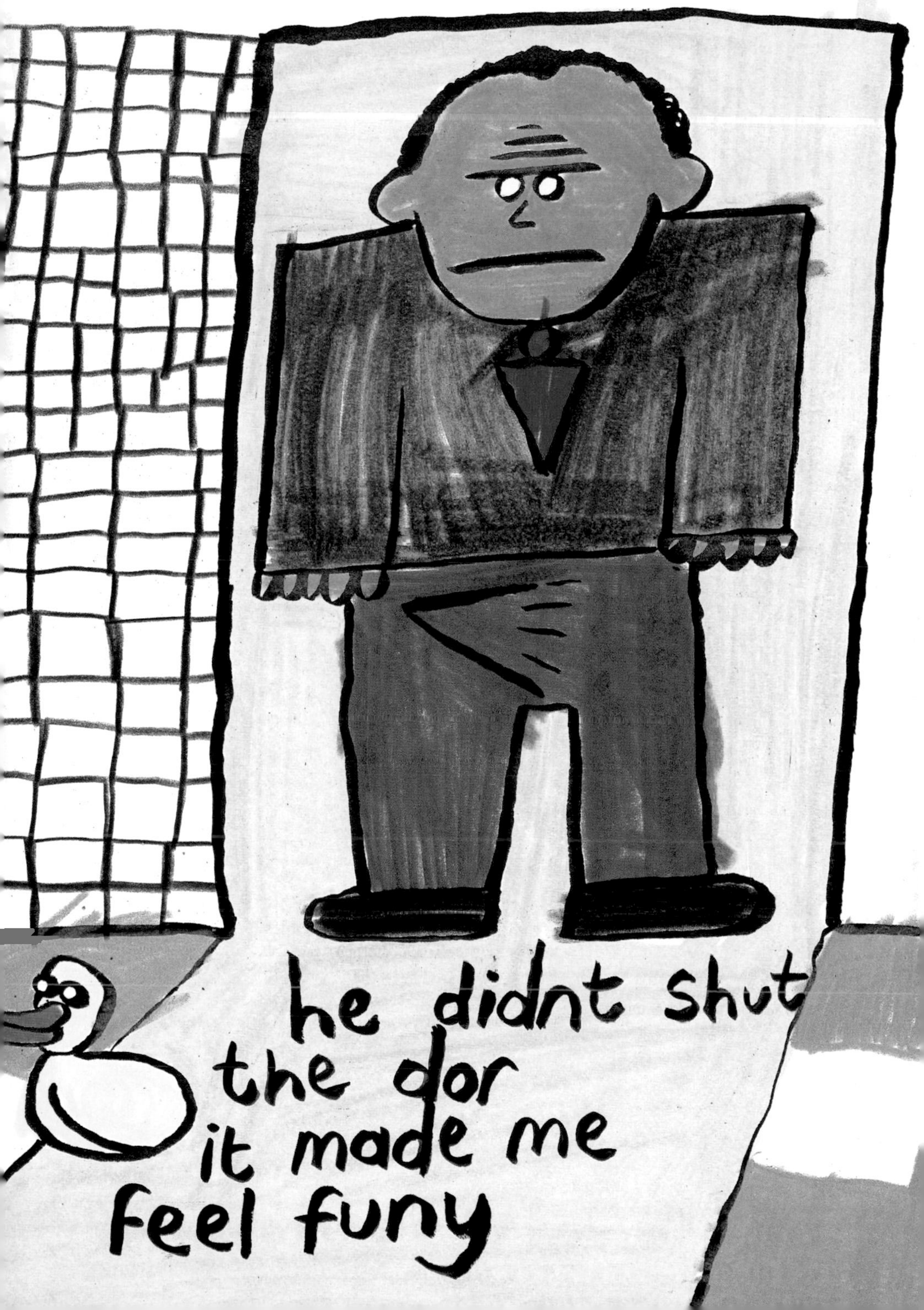
he didnt shut
the dor
it made me
feel funy

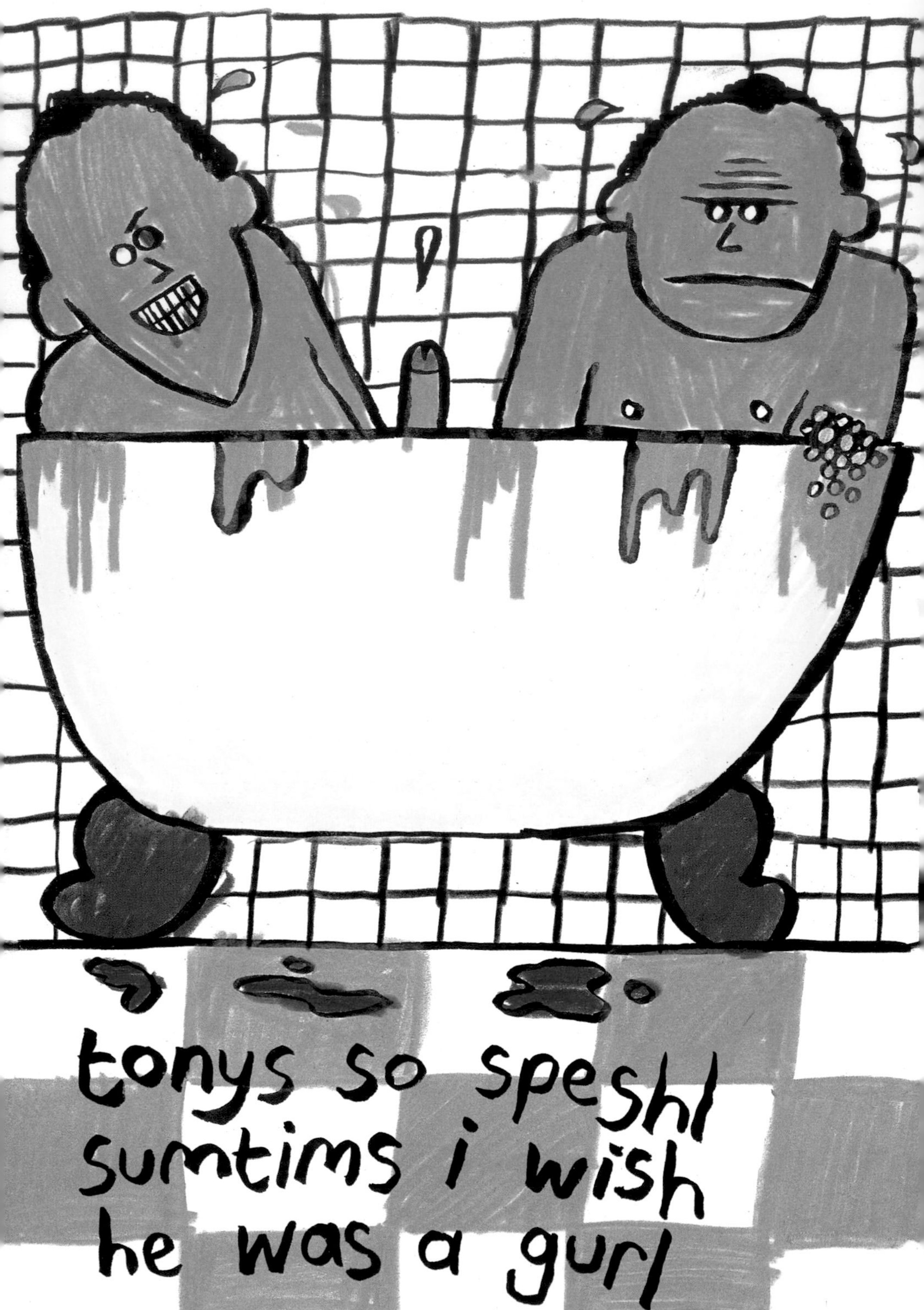
tonys so speshl
sumtims i wish
he was a gurl

puzzl joyn the dots + culer in

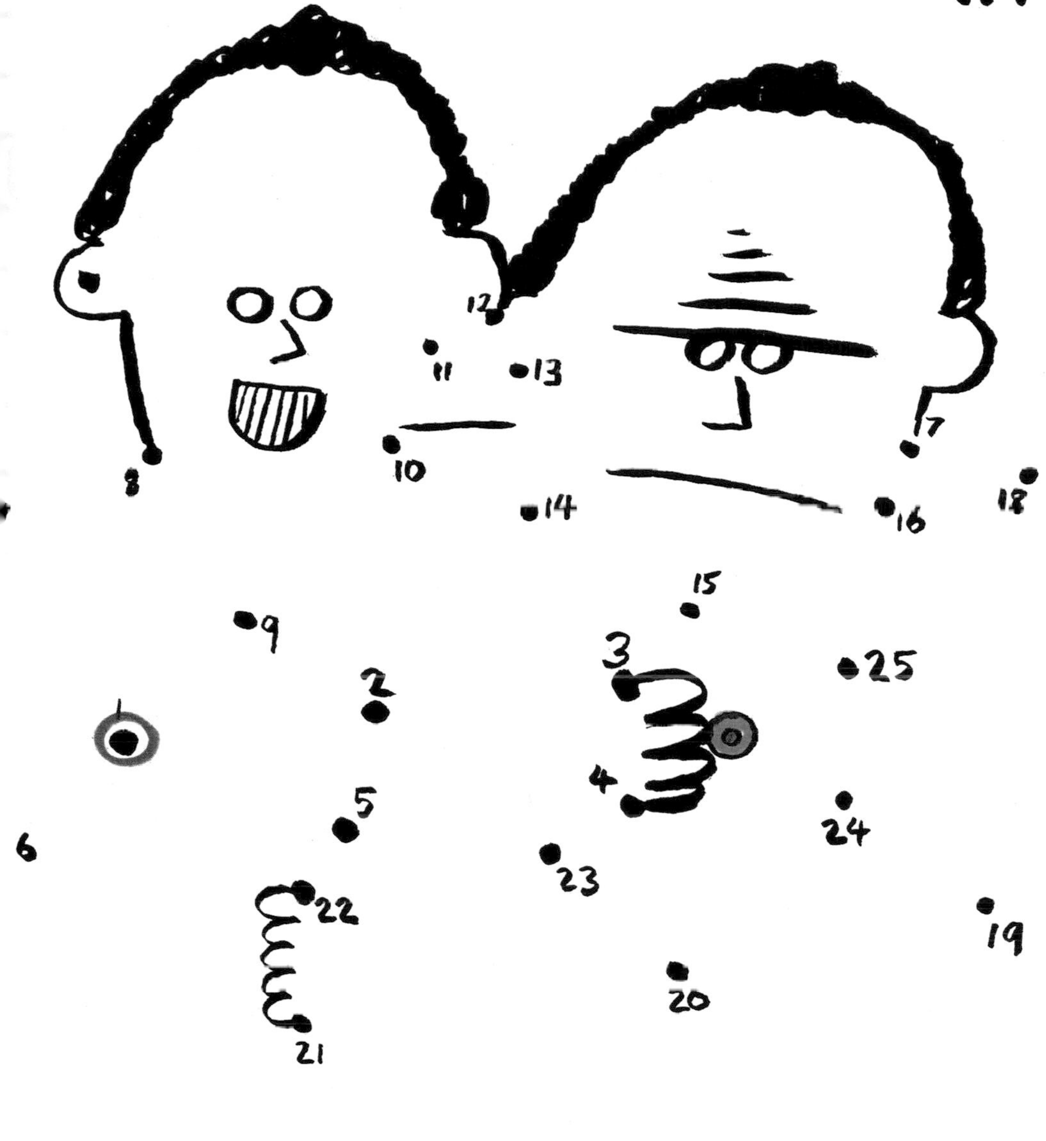

its tony tuchin my nipl

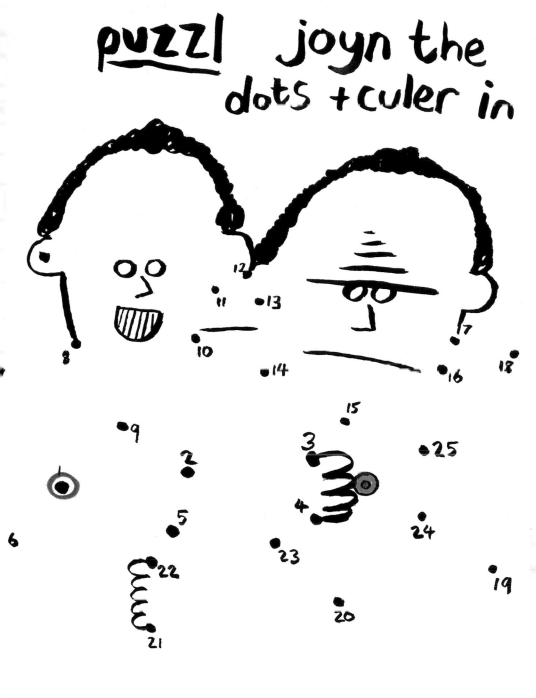

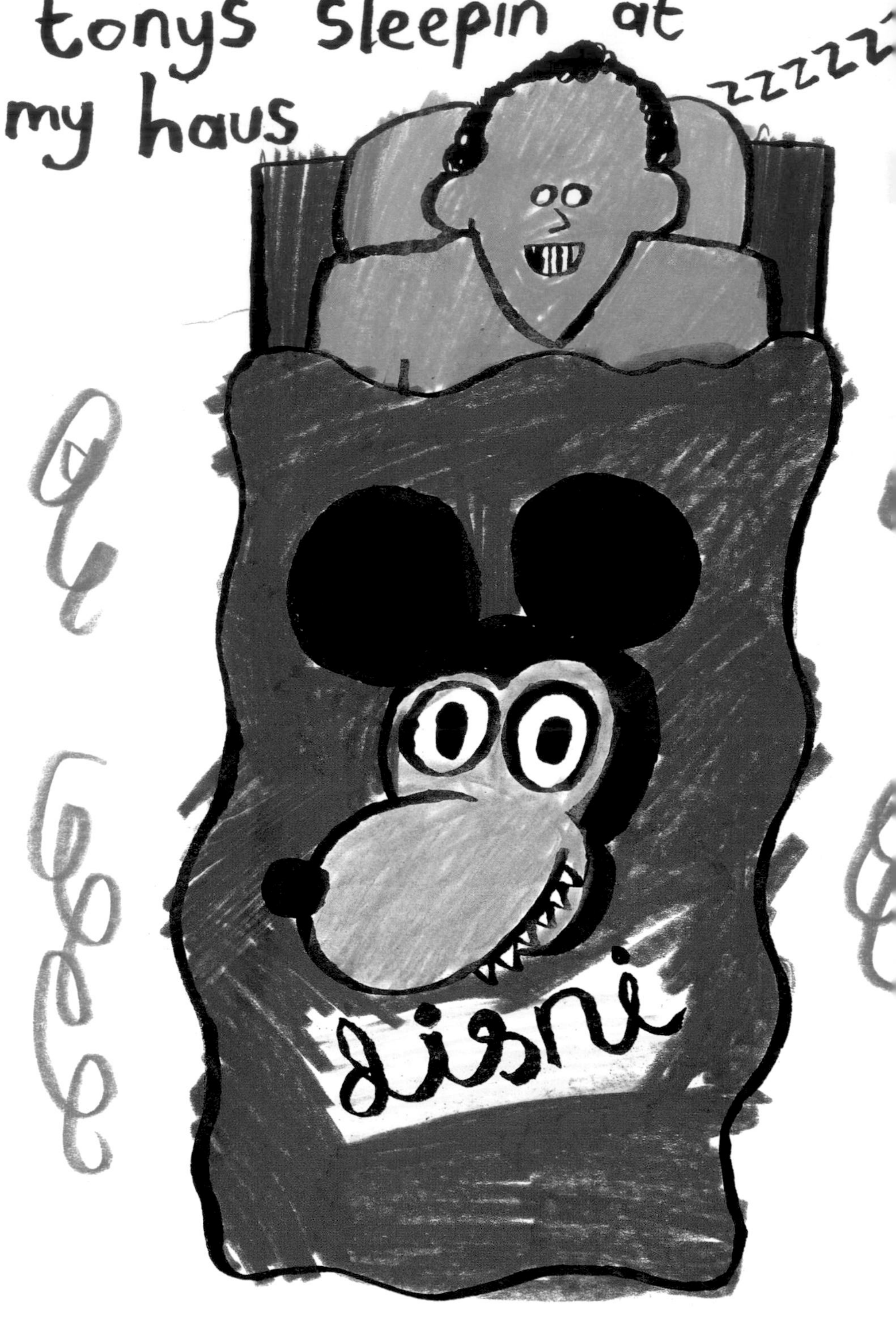
tonys sleepin at my haus
zzzzzz
disni

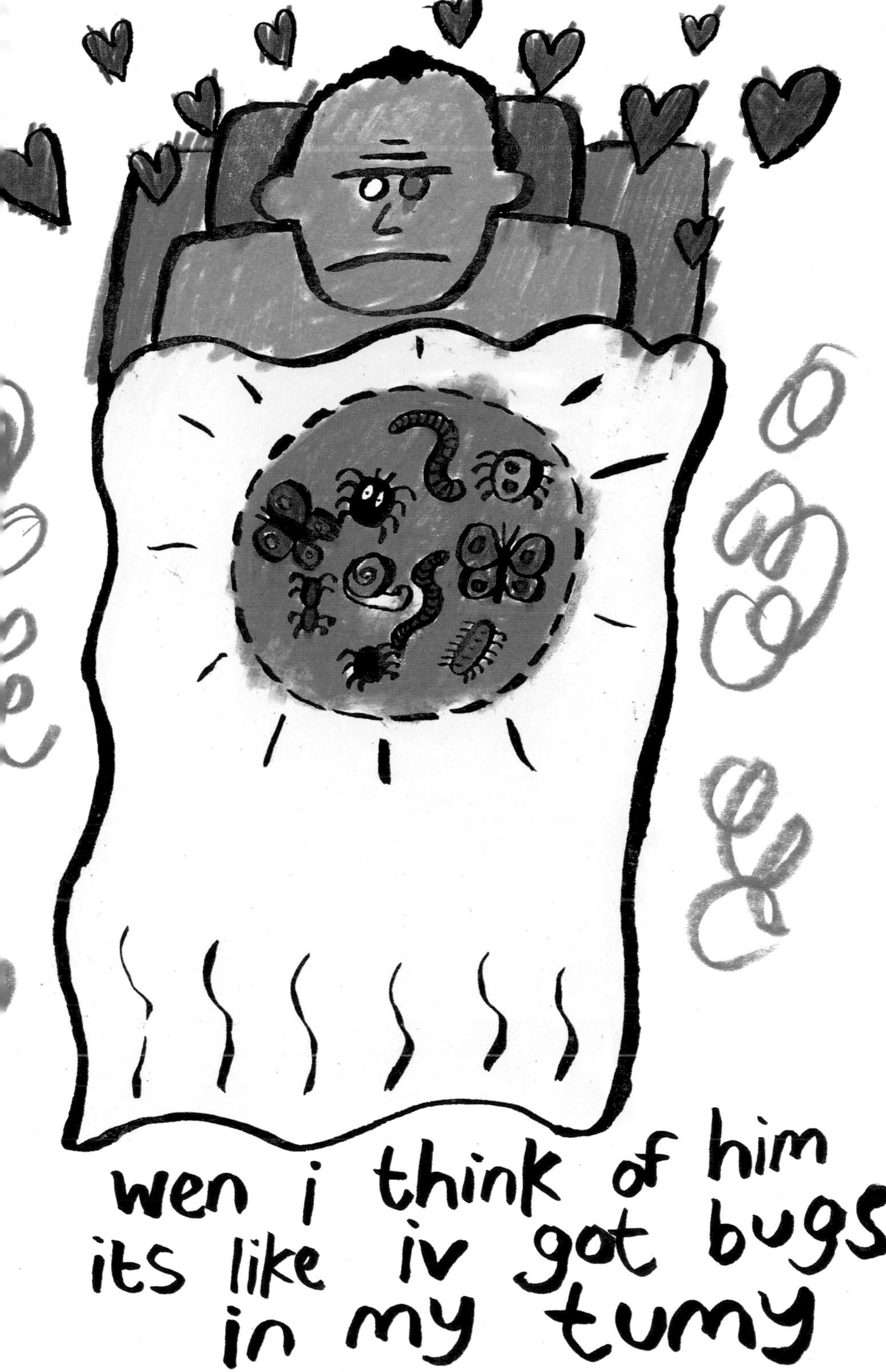

wen i think of him its like iv got bugs in my tumy

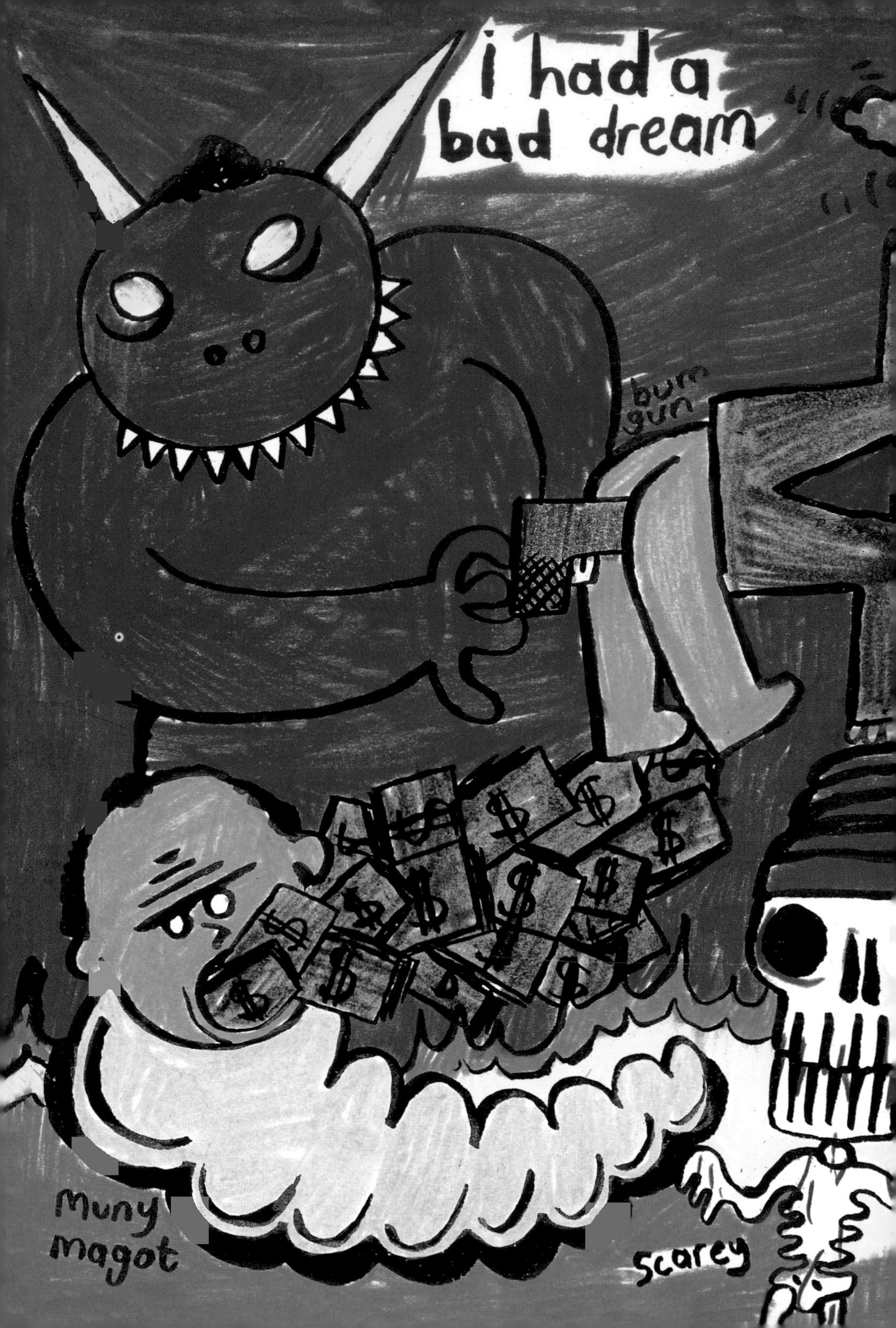
i had a bad dream
bum gun
muny magot
scarey

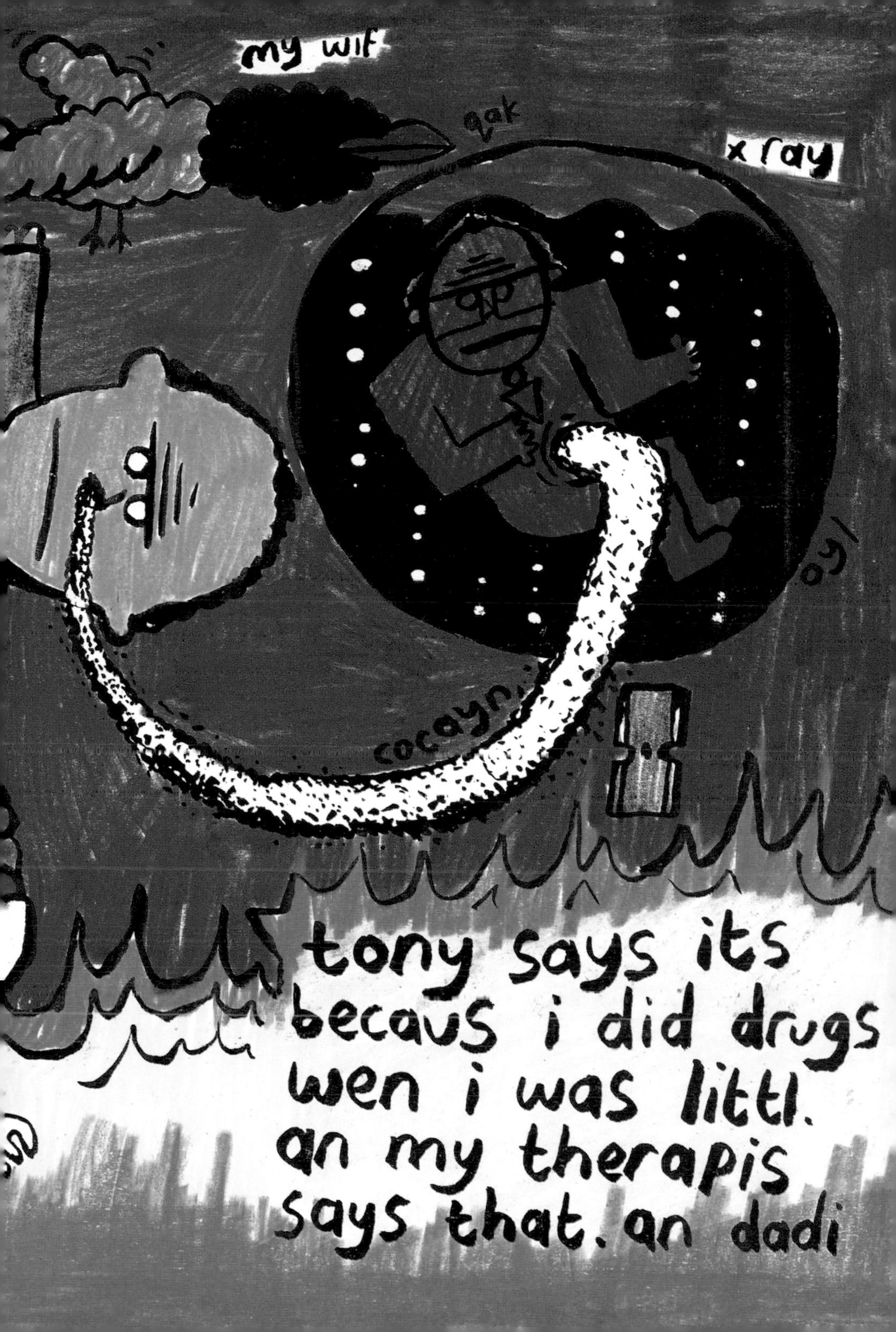
my wif
qak
x ray
oyl
cocayn
tony says its
becaus i did drugs
wen i was littl.
an my therapis
says that. an dadi

me an tony play hide the choclat

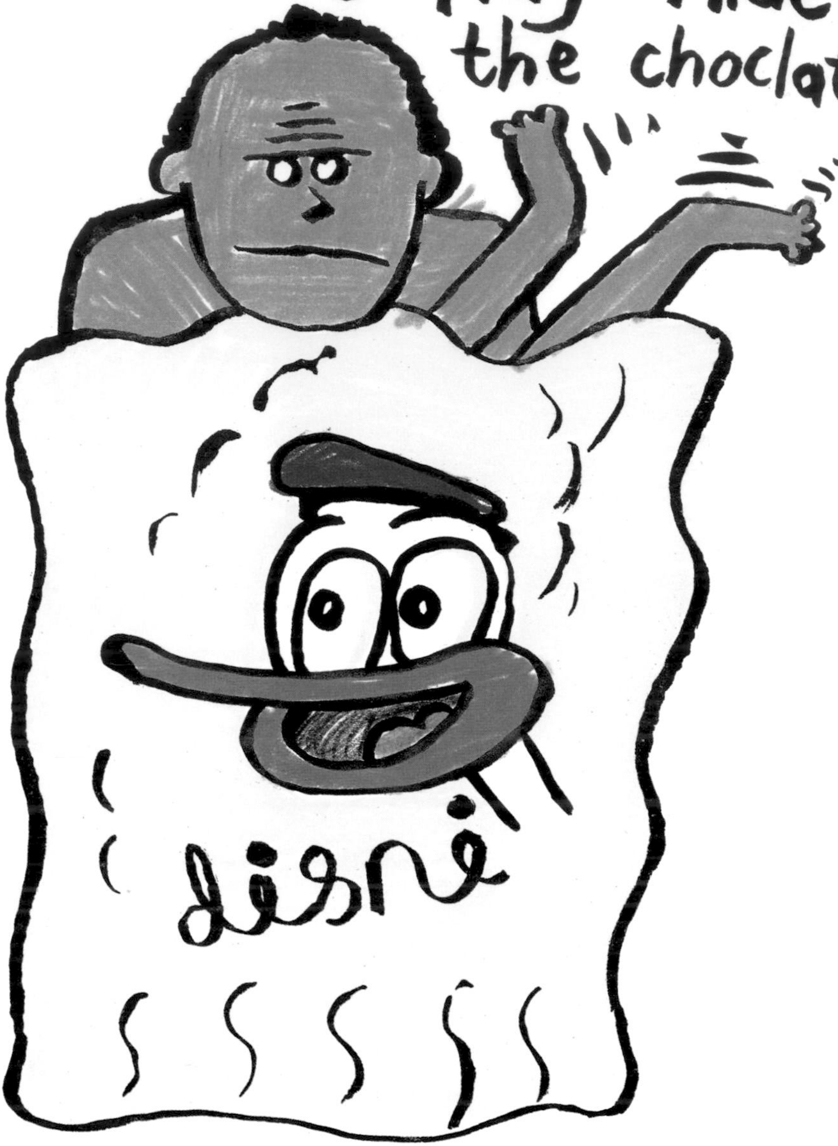
disne

i won

culerin in pitur

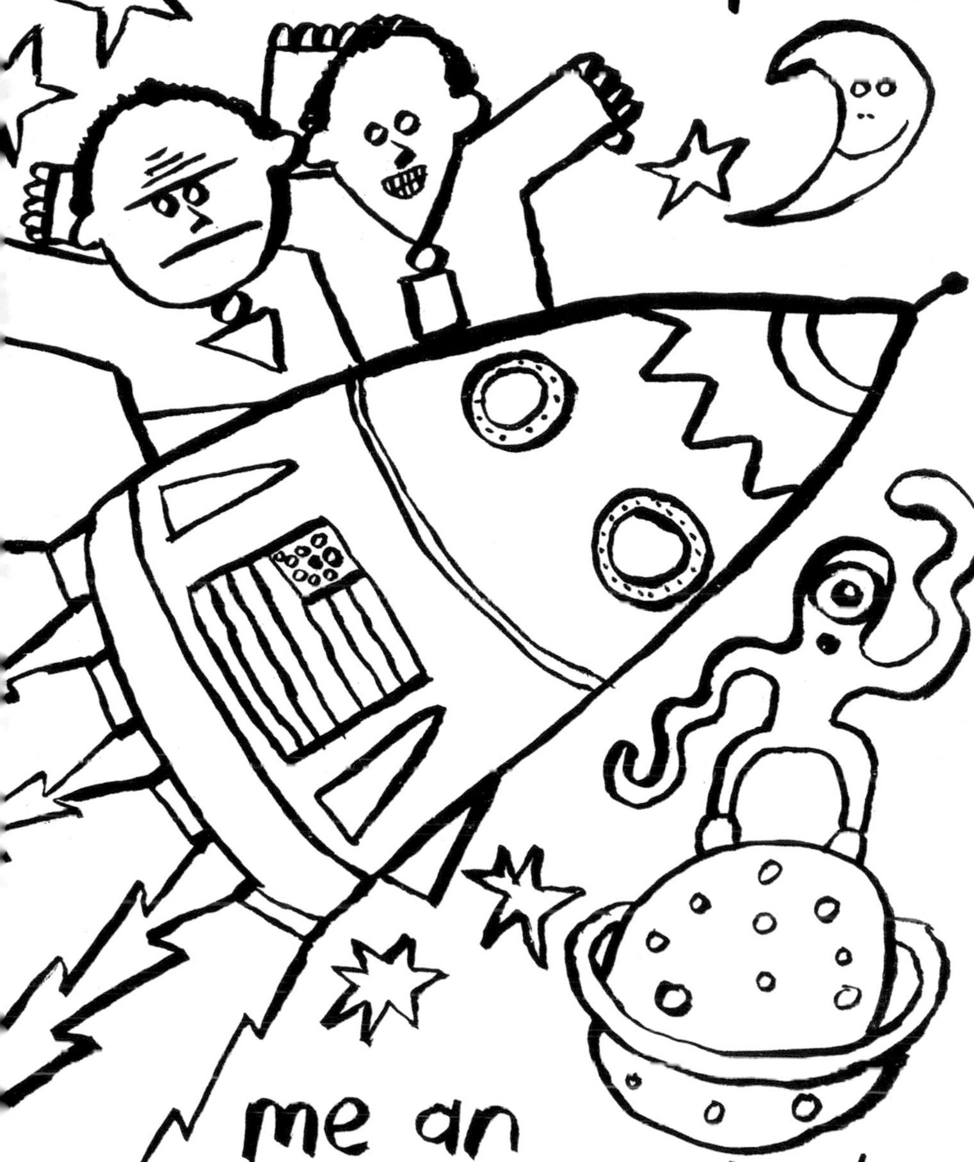

me an
tony are goin to
liv in Spas

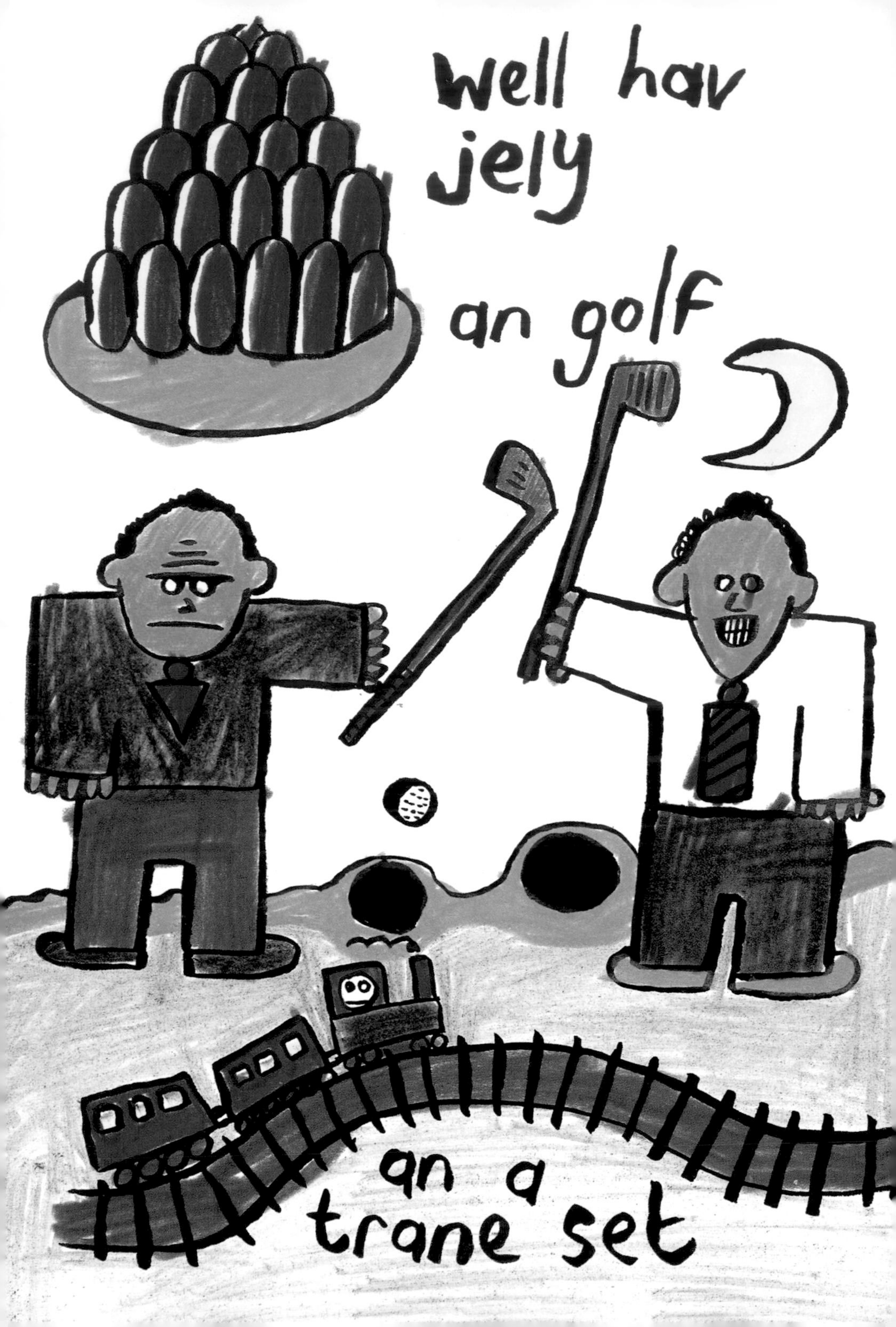
well hav
jely
an golf
an a
trane set

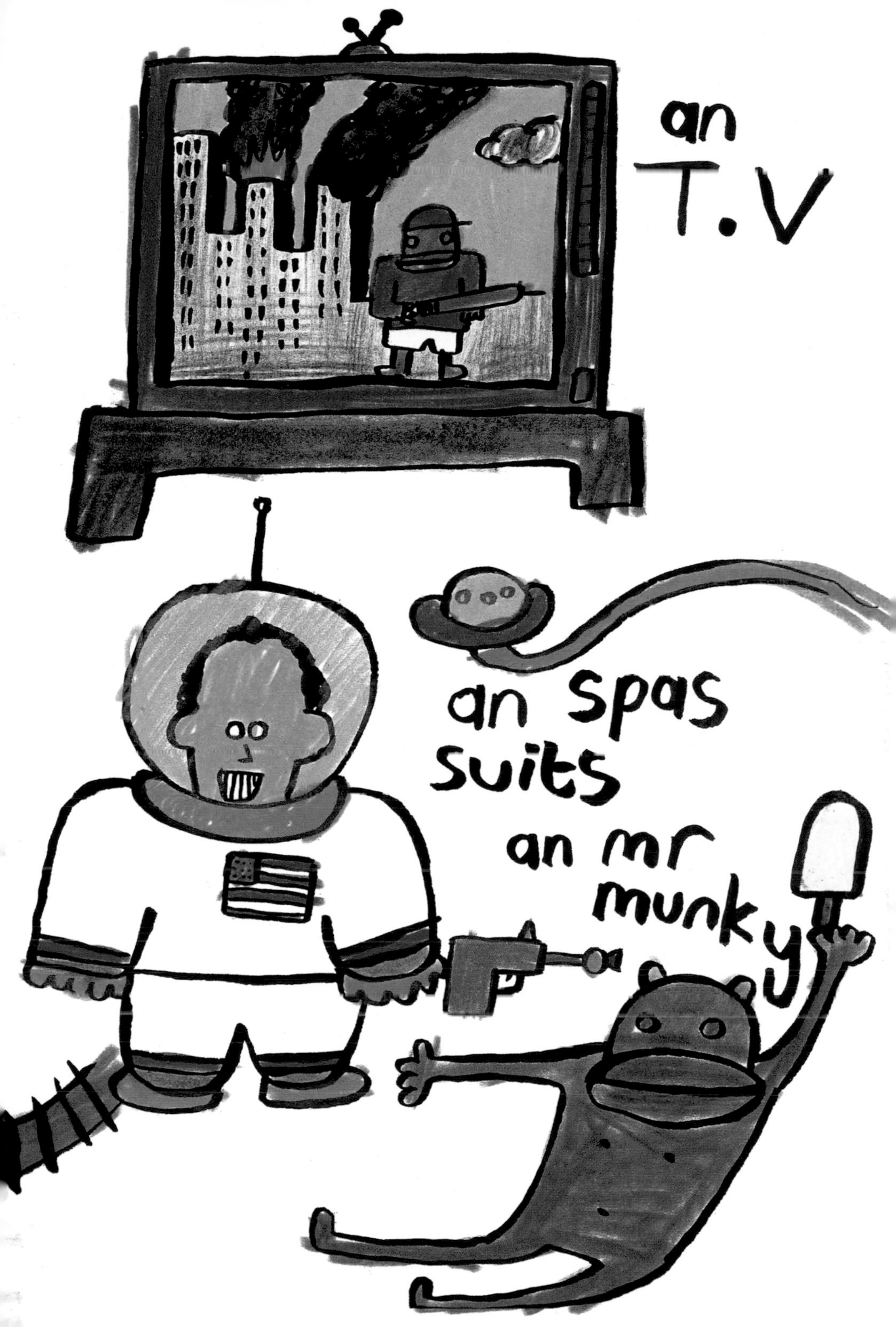
an
T.V
an spas
suits
an mr
munky

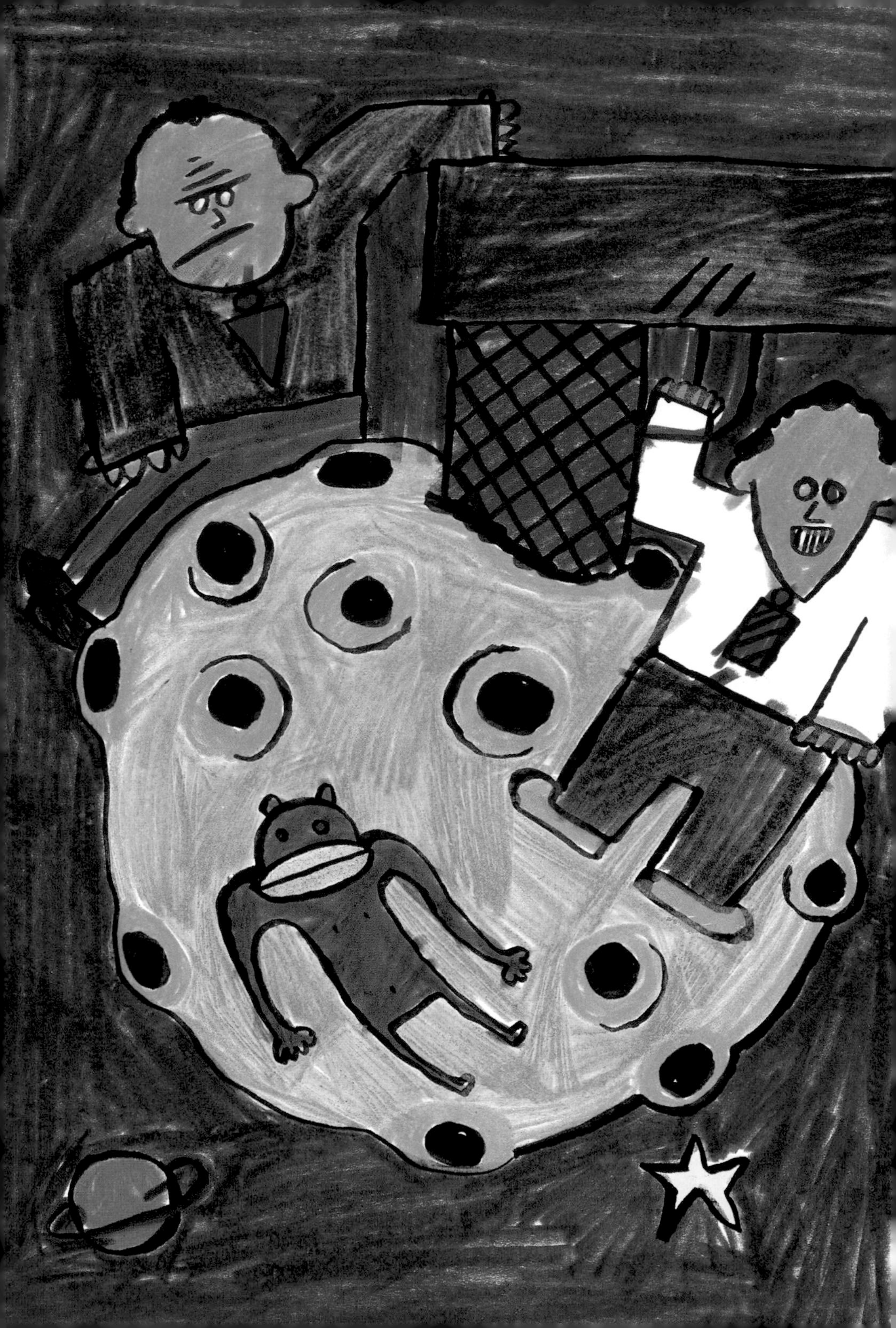

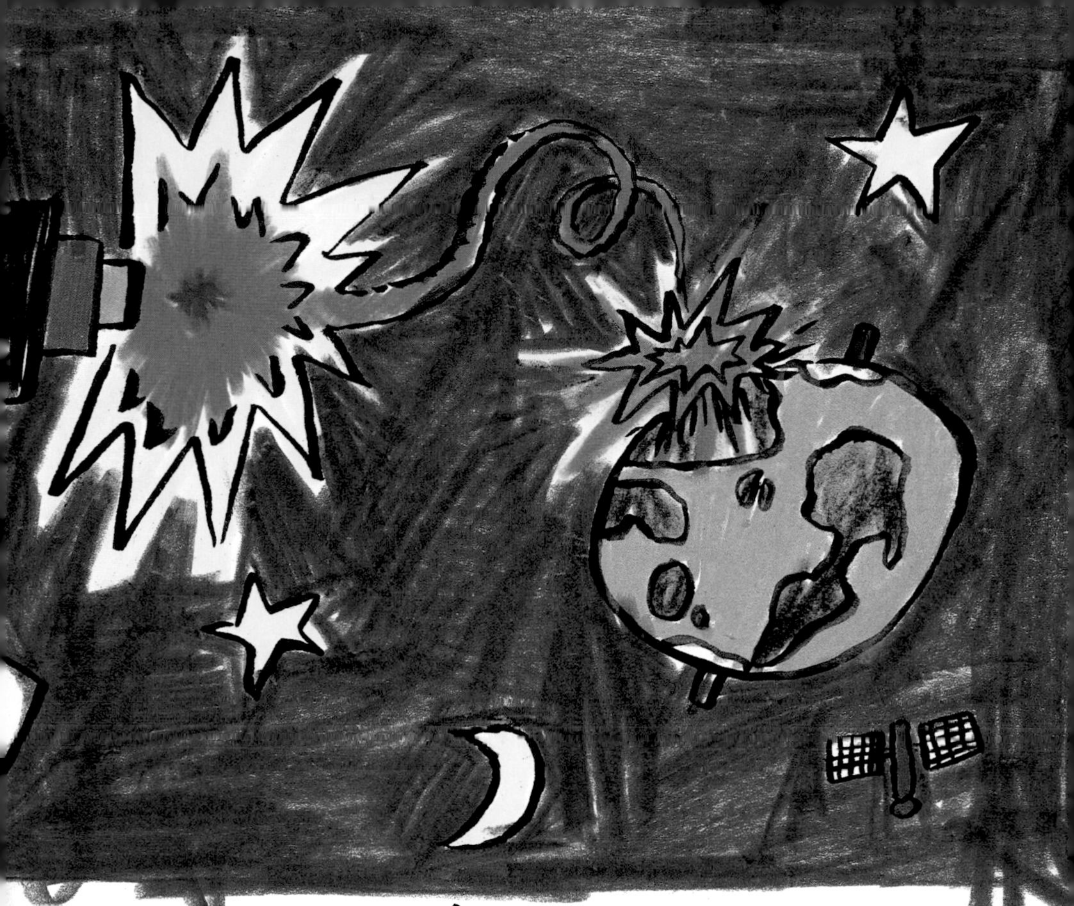

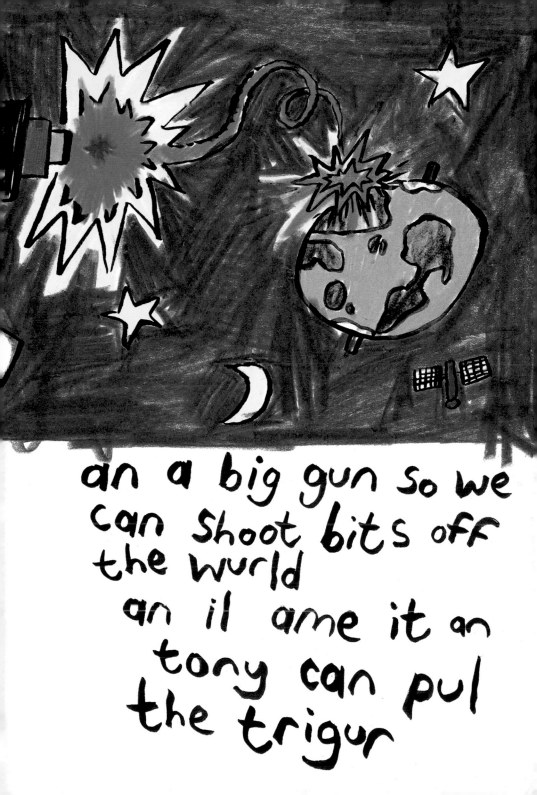

an a big gun so we
can shoot bits off
the wurld
an il ame it an
tony can pul
the trigur

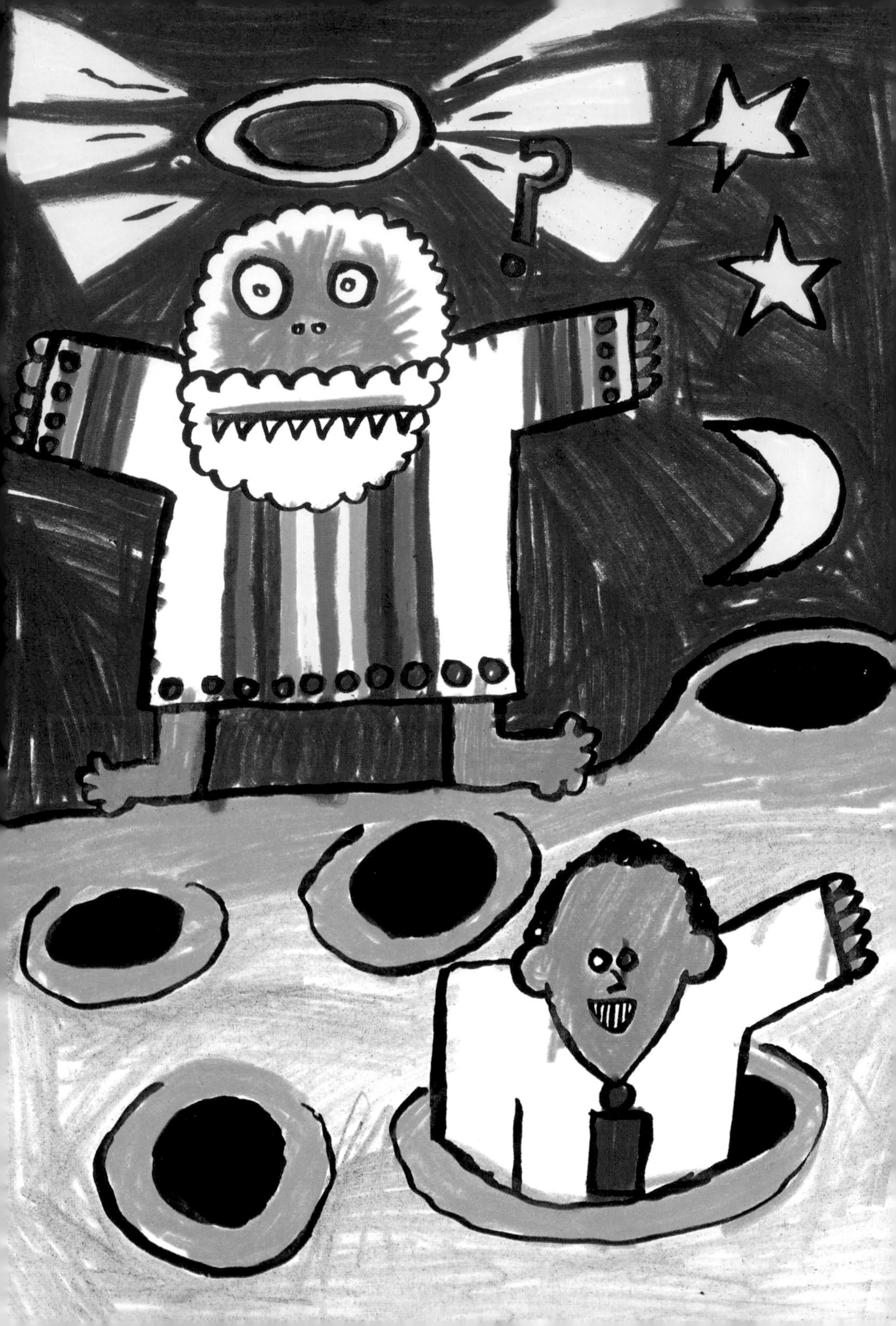

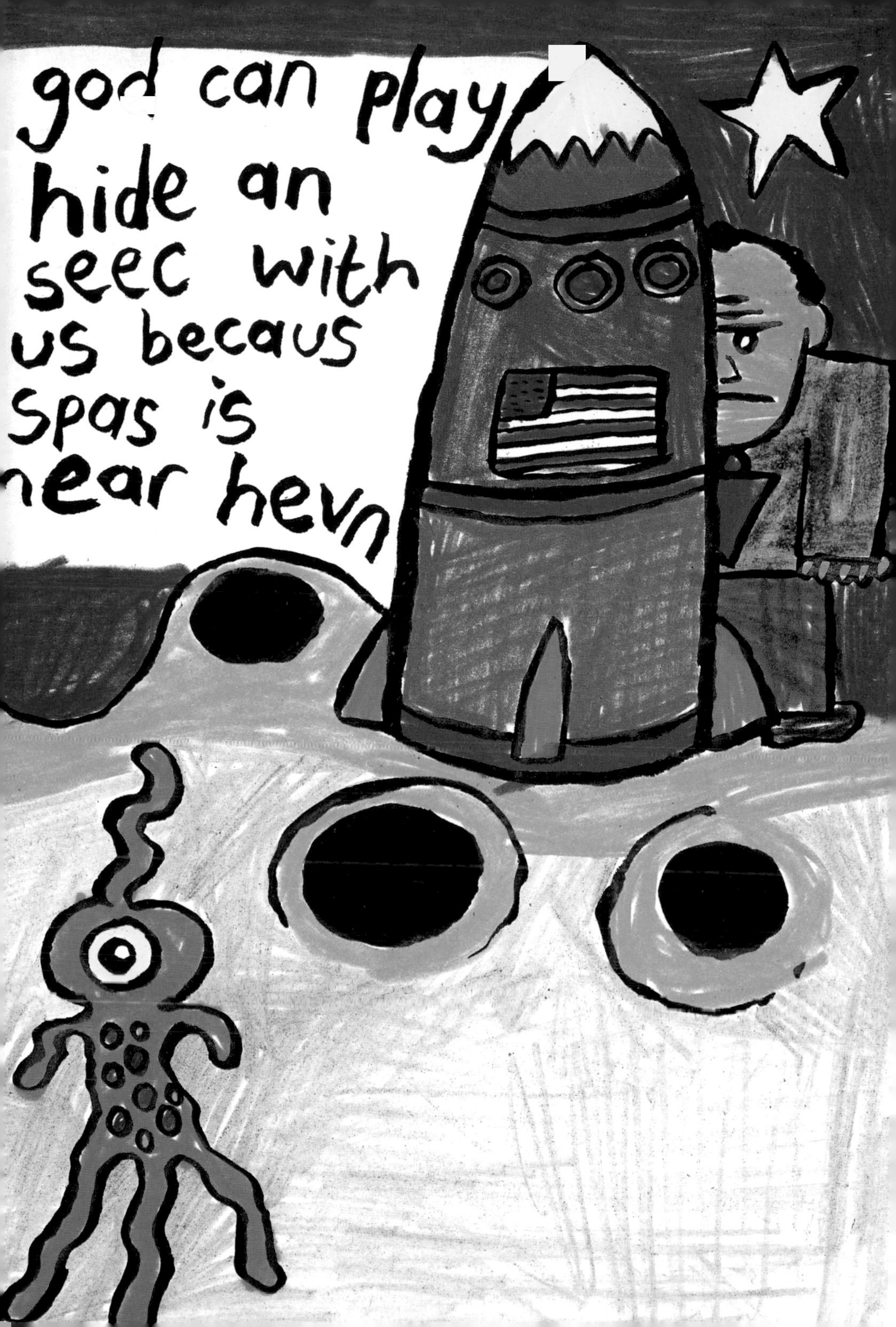
god can play
hide an
seec with
us becaus
spas is
near hevn

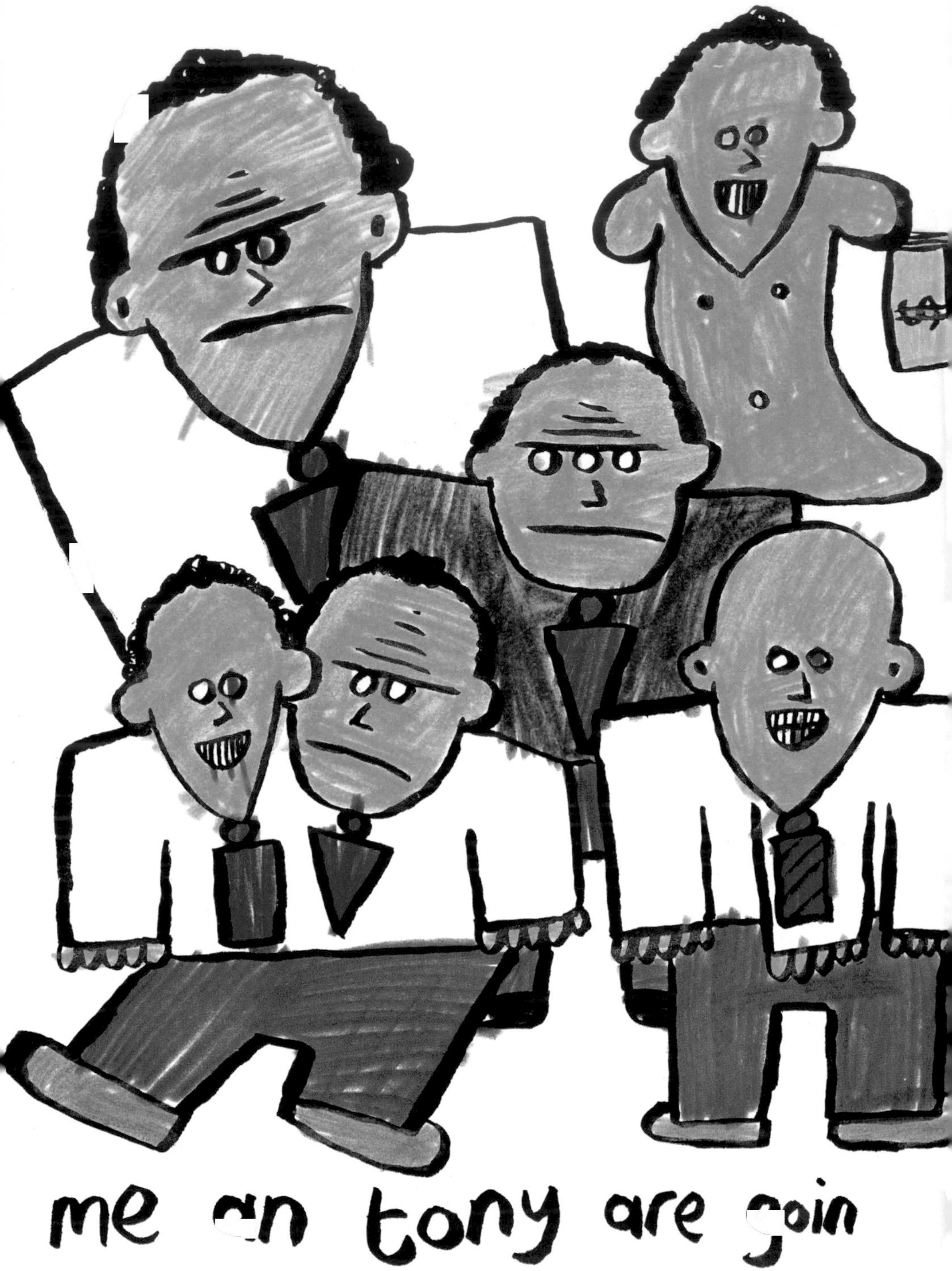

me an tony are goin

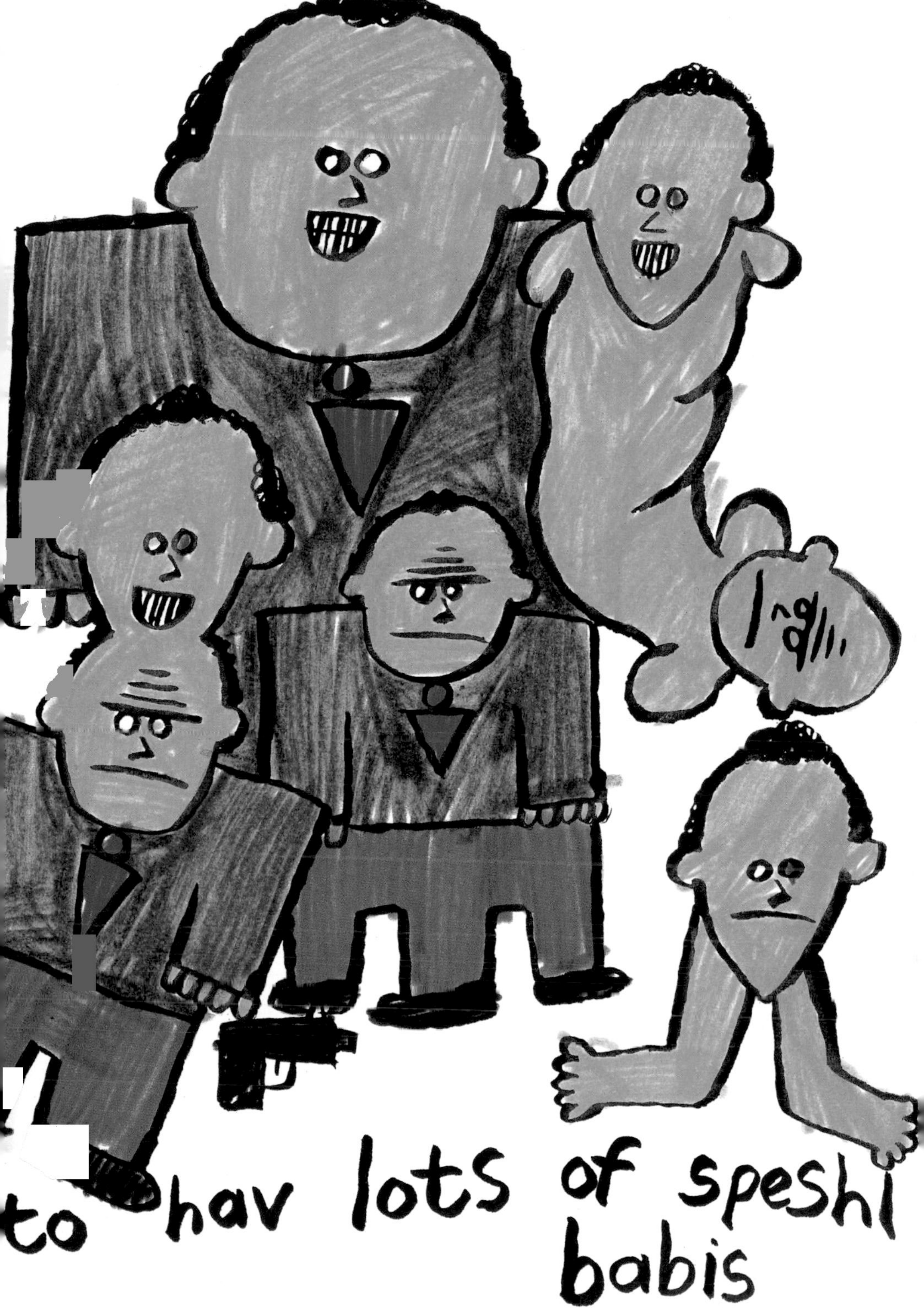

to hav lots of speshl babis

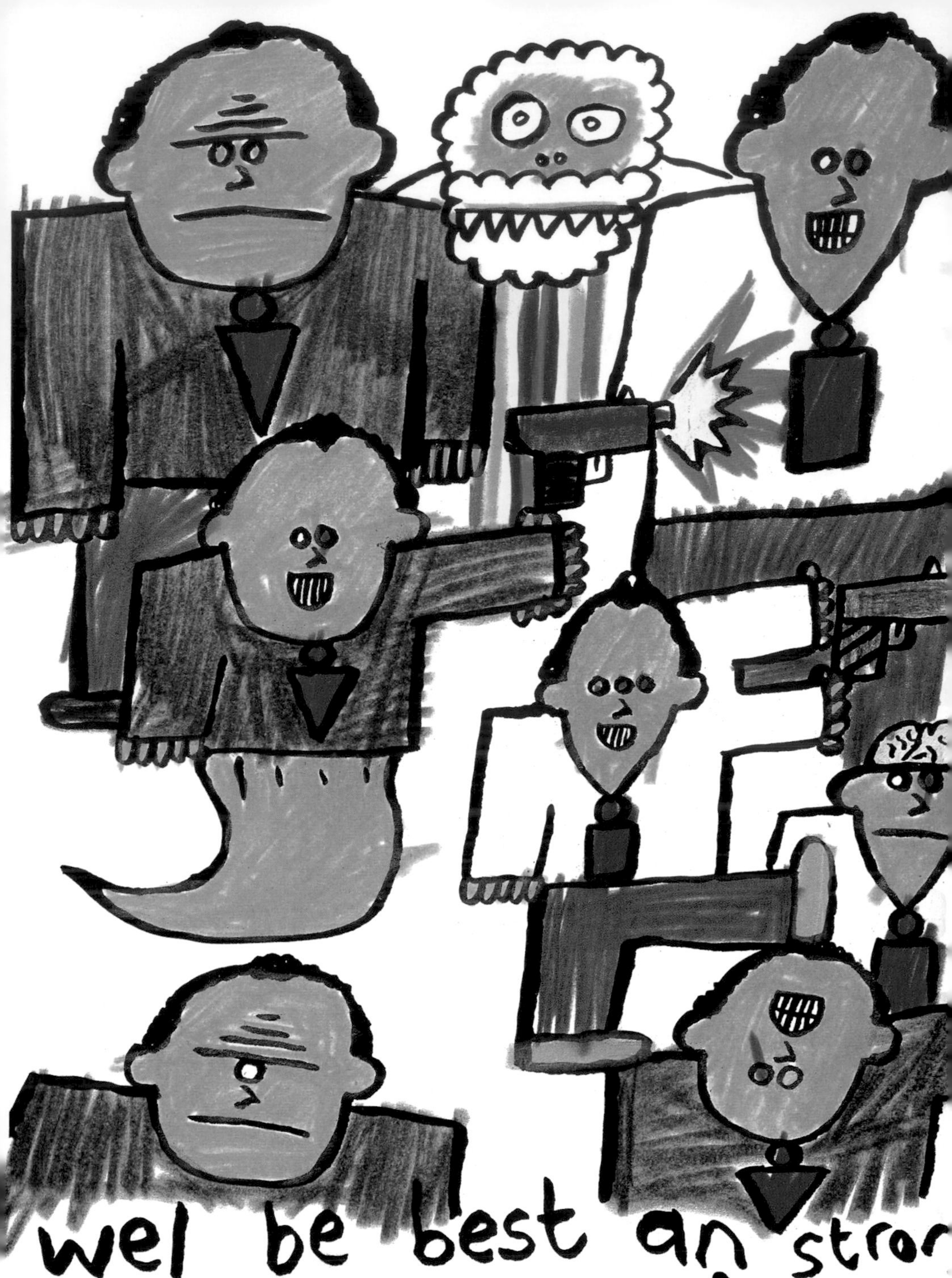

wel be best an stron
to stop US my babi

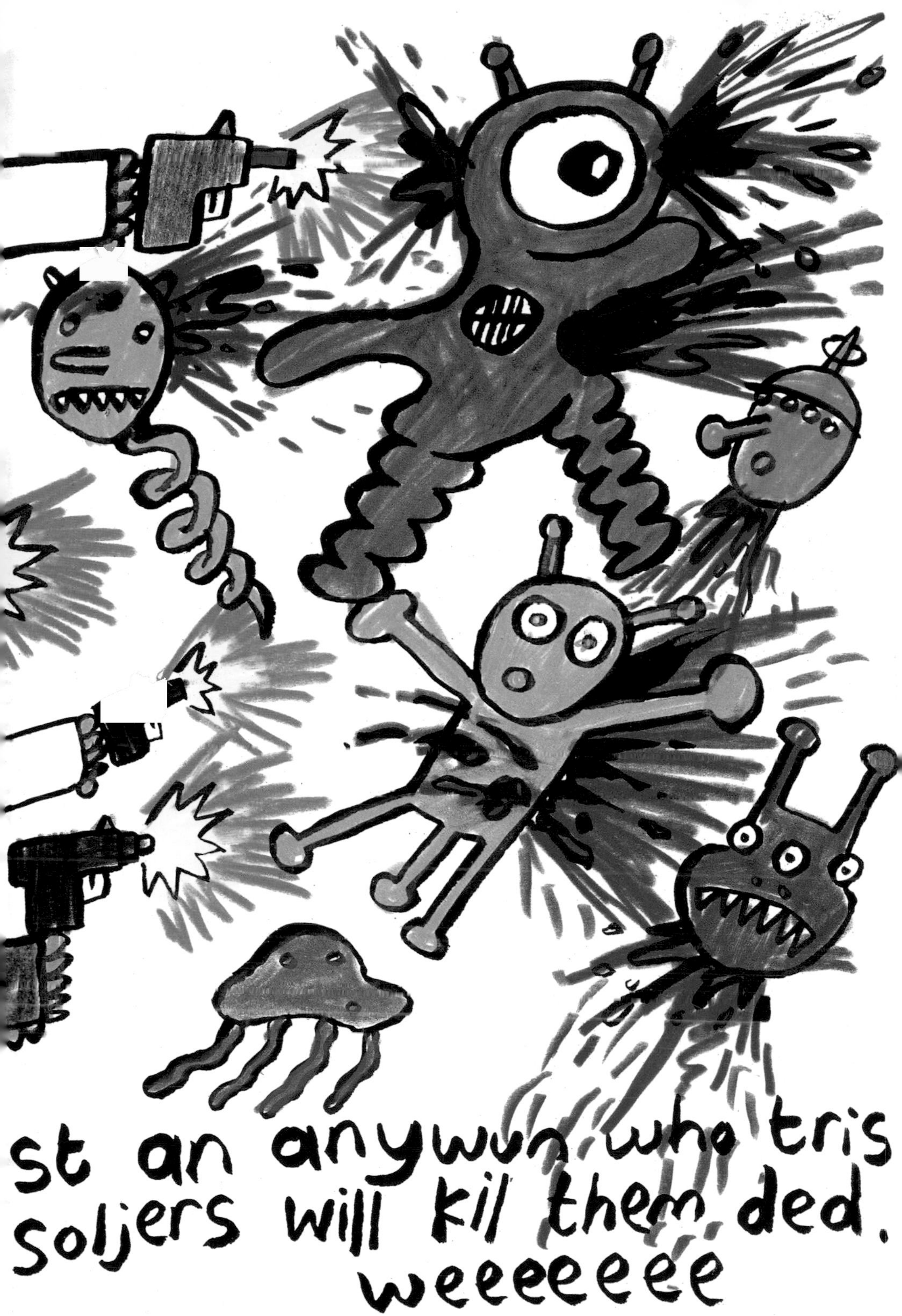

st an anywun who tris
soljers will kil them ded.
weeeeeee

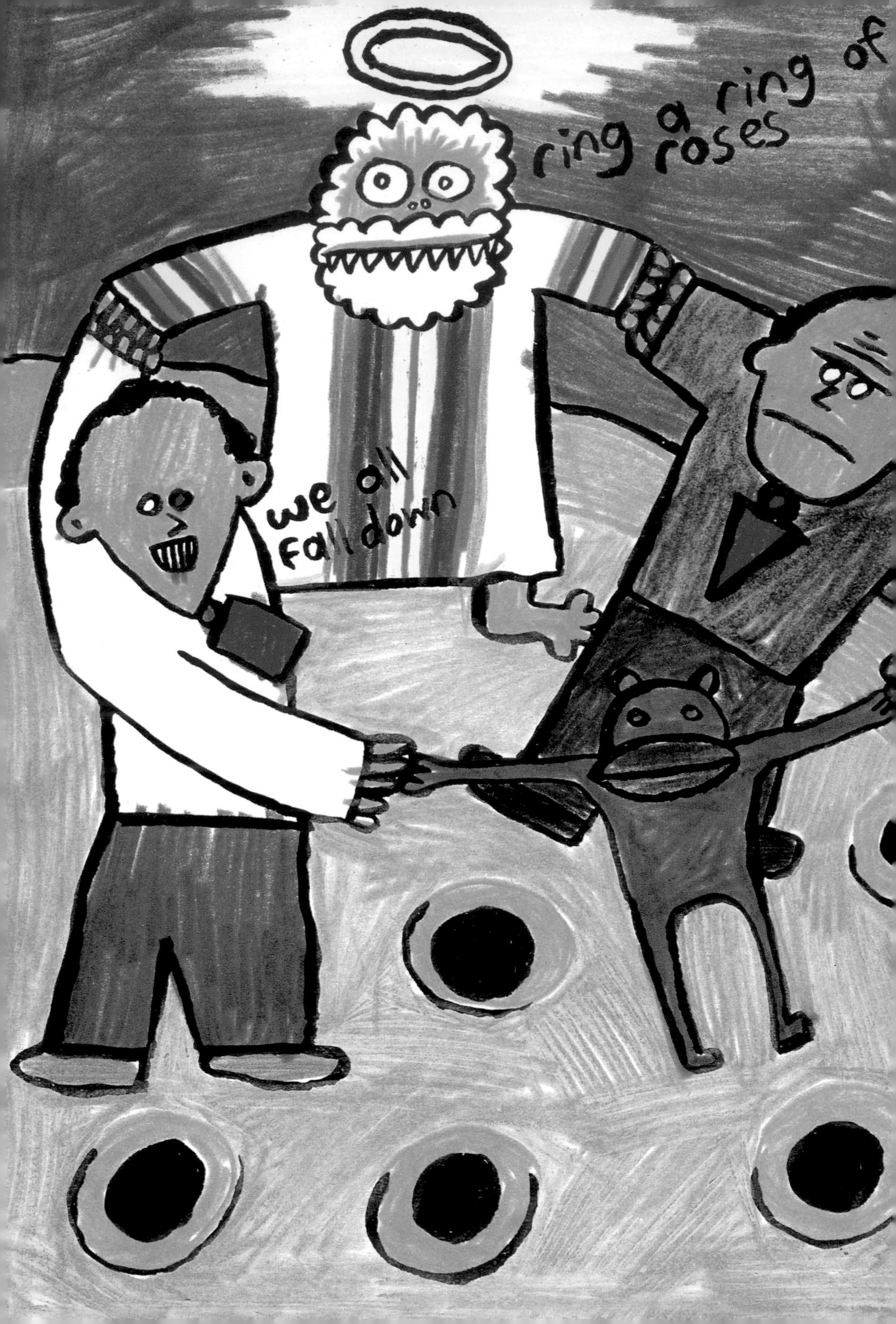
ring a ring of roses
we all fall down

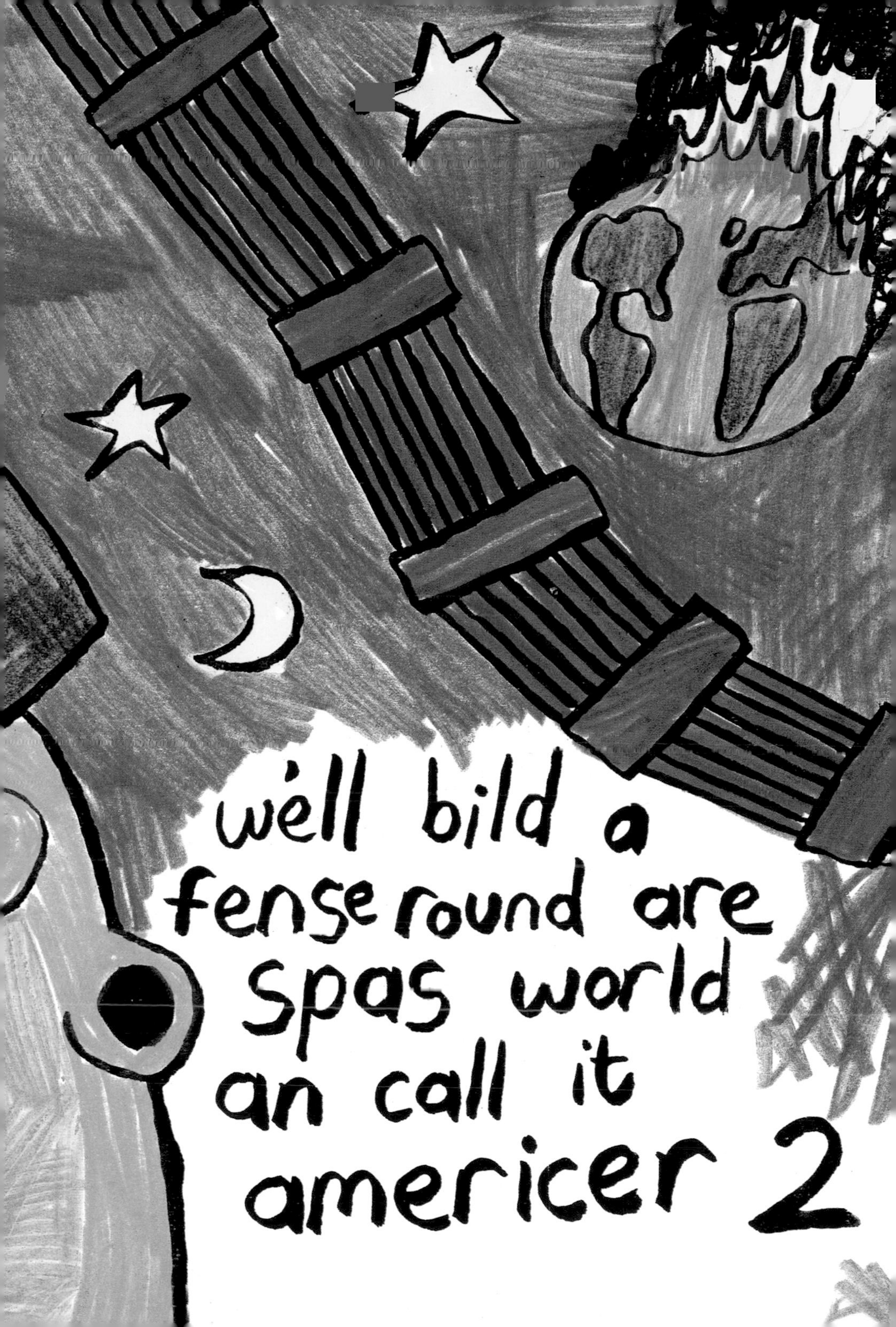
wėll bild a
fense round are
spas world
an call it
americer 2

an it dusnt mattr
if noone likes it becau
theyl all be ded

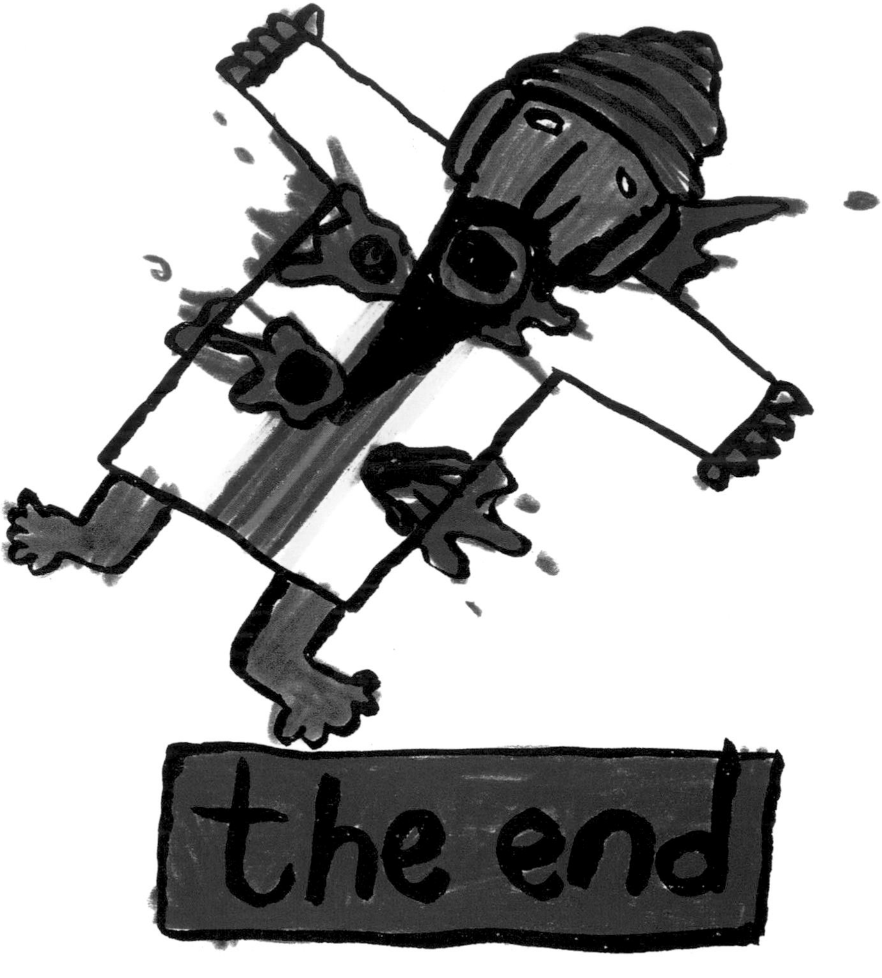
the end

www.drparsons.co.uk

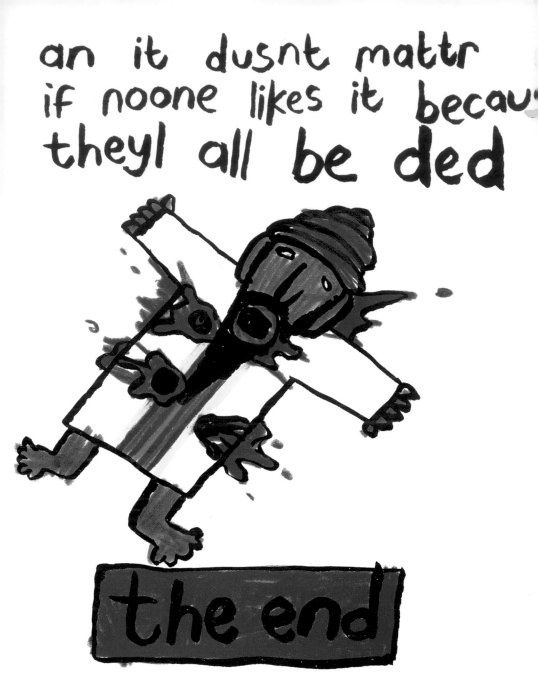